THE PRACTICAL PRIMARY DRAMA HANDBOOK

THE PRACTICAL PRIMARY DRAMA HANDBOOK

Patrice Baldwin

Los Angeles • London • New Delhi • Singapore

First published 2008

SAGE Publications Ltd
1 Oliver's Yard
55 City Road
London EC1Y 1SP

SAGE Publications Inc
2455 Teller Road
Thousand Oaks, California 91320

SAGE Publications India Pvt Ltd
B 1/I 1 Mohan Cooperative Industrial Area
Mathura Road,
New Delhi 110 044

SAGE Publications Asia-Pacific Pte Ltd
33 Pekin Street #02-01
Far East Square
Singapore 048763

Library of Congress Control Number: 2007942818

British Library Cataloguing in Publication Data

A catalogue record for this book is available from the British Library

ISBN 978-1-4129-2964-6
ISBN 978-1-4129-2965-3 (pbk)

Typeset by C&M Digitals (P) Ltd, Chennai, India
Printed in India by Replika Press, Pvt. Ltd
Printed on paper from sustainable resources

CONTENTS

Acknowledgements

Illustrations by Garry Parsons from *Billy's Bucket* by Kes Gray, published by Bodley Head. Reprinted by permission of The Random House Group Ltd.

Photographs of London reprinted by permission of the Museum of London Picture Library.

Photography by Egyptian expedition, The Metropolitan Museum of Art, Image © The Metropolitan Museum of Art.

CHAPTER 1

Drama in Schools – Some Basic Questions Answered

What do we mean by drama in schools?

Drama in schools ideally includes:

- free and supported dramatic play opportunities

- drama lessons within which children are taught how to do drama itself

- the use of drama methodology in lessons other than just English and drama

- whole-class drama lessons through which children explore issues and ideas together (learning in and across curriculum areas)

- opportunities to create, perform and respond to their own and each other's performances

- opportunities to create, perform and respond to professional theatre performances (including theatre visits in schools)

- participatory opportunities to work creatively and evaluatively with actors and playwrights.

There is much confusion about what 'drama in schools' includes. Drama should be seen by schools as much more than just putting on the Christmas play or acting out scenes in assembly. It should also include opportunities for working and learning in role regularly together in group and whole-class situations.

Some schools will include the provision of dramatic play opportunities, which involve being in role, as part of what they define as drama. To make drama in schools only playing *or* plays, would deprive many children of the rich spectrum of experience and possibilities that can be offered through both *learning in drama* and *learning through drama* with whole classes.

Role play and pretending is natural and essential to the all round development of young children and a powerful educational opportunity is missed if children do not have an opportunity to move from their own pre-school role play into 'in-school' role play and then whole-class drama/role play at school, as well as the important experience of participating in performances.

What do we mean by 'whole-class drama'?

Whole-class drama should be done *with* children not *to* them. The term 'whole-class drama' refers to the whole class working in role together within one overall, shared, fiction that they are creating and contributing to together, in order to make it work.

Whole-class drama can split into groups working in role or solitary working in role at times, but it will also involve the whole class spontaneously interacting in role together, in the same scenes for significant amounts of the time. They are all involved in the same overall drama even when they are working in role individually or in groups, for example, we might ask the class to create scenes in groups that portray what has happened to a character at different points in the past and then bring the groups' scenes together to build up missing bits of the plot (for example, Unit 7, Activity 4 and Unit 8, Activity 10, at the end of this book). The scenes would be complementary and contribute to the evolving whole-class drama. The whole class is engaging with and offering parts of the same collaborative fiction, with the structural guidance and and co-participative support of the teacher. The teacher herself/himself is likely to be working as a co-participant in role for much of the time but can step out of role whenever required, to organize the lesson or give instructions as the teacher.

Why is role play and drama important for every child?

In every culture in the world young children who are developing normally will pretend. They will do this because their brains need the opportunity to imagine and because they enjoy pretending! Because the brain needs to pretend, it makes the activity enjoyable, to make sure it happens. So, dramatic play and drama are naturally highly motivating to young children. Before entering school, they spend a great deal of their time naturally and spontaneously role-playing alone and with others.

When they get to school they often are given very limited opportunities to role-play even though their developing brain needs it. Their brains are wired up to learn through actively reliving and imagining experiences, at first alone and then with other children. To be able to pretend involves drama skills, and children already bring them to school. For educators not to use this natural method of learning once children arrive in schools would seem foolish, and could even be construed as a form of deprivation. With children entering nurseries and schools earlier, and with children spending more time at schools and with the extended school day, it is essential that they do not lose the opportunity for spontaneous and imaginative play, both alone and with others.

There is evidence to suggest that the brain changes structurally in response to what it experiences. The time when language is developing most rapidly and when the brain's pathways for learning (neural pathways) are being connected up is the same time in children's lives when they are most frequently pretending through dramatic play. This is no coincidence. Imagined worlds that they imitate, re-enact or create can give them an infinite range of contexts within which they can practise speaking and actively listening. In dramas and role plays they can speak and respond as anyone conjured up from their own imaginations and experience. They can imagine themselves to be anywhere at any point in time with anything happening.

When left to their own dramatic play, without an empathetic adult intervening, children tend to repeat the same play rather than learn new things. They tend to enact and move speedily through plots without much time for conscious reflection. But with an empathetic adult alongside who has a learning agenda for them and who has some knowledge of basic drama strategies, children can be encouraged to engage more deeply with sustained learning through the pretend. Also they can be supported to sustain a collective exploration with other children that might otherwise be inclined to break down earlier socially. With an adult they can enter playfully, yet seriously, into new learning territory.

Drama as multi-sensory learning

The brain learns multi-sensorily. Dramatic play (and later good drama) enables children to operate multi-sensorily, rather than rely on learning mainly through reading, writing and listening to teachers. Drama like dramatic play is visual, auditory, kinaesthetic and tactile. It involves children being physically and mentally active, being on the move, interacting and responding to each other for a social and learning purpose and, above all, thinking. Whole-class drama is readily accessible to a wide range of types of learner as it resonates with earlier, familiar dramatic play. Older children, too, still value working in role as it is highly motivational and many older children are covertly dramatic playing outside school for years longer than most adults realize. Of course, adults, too, still play dramatically from time to time. If you are going to make a speech you might rehearse in front of an imaginary audience. If you have an interview you might practise in front of a mirror. You might even employ fantasy and role play as an adult to excite another. You can know that you are pretending but the emotions and learning are real.

Drama as socialization

To keep a 'pretend' going with others, children need to pay attention to each other, listen and watch each other, and negotiate and co-operate. In carrying out a make-believe with others, children show what they already know. It gives us an insight into what children have already experienced and understood (or misunderstood) and helps us know what we need to help them to learn next. Working alongside children sensitively and empathetically in role provides educators with a powerful and engaging way of keeping interactively alongside children as they learn and helps to structure learning and to mediate experience. The teacher using drama in schools can be seen as a natural development of the playful and empathetic parent or carer, who quite naturally is drawn to play alongside children in their pretend worlds. Within those worlds the alert adult becomes aware of a myriad of unfolding learning opportunities for both the children and themselves.

Drama as empathy

Being in role encourages the development of empathy and this helps children to understand and feel other people's positions and viewpoints. Children can respond in role to unfamiliar situations and practise and rehearse how to deal with real ones. Drama situations may portray real-life situations that have been experienced or may be invented. However, invented situations are always in some way rooted in the real-life experiences of the child as they draw on what they already know (or have seen or heard about) in order to create drama. It is one of the reasons child psychologists are observant of children's pretend play. But we do need to remember that through television children pick up on much to imitate that may not be in their direct experience. Also teachers are not psychologists and drama in schools never sets out to be psychodrama (which is a specialist area).

Drama as freedom

When we operate in role, the make-believe is liberating. Working in role provides a possible distance and a safety net that enables participants to attach and detach themselves at will, to step in or out of role and disassociate themselves personally from what they said or did as a character. Dramatic play, drama and theatre is a magical play space that we agree to keep going together and be experientially playful in, but when the make-believe finishes the characters in the make-believe (however real they may have seemed) have vanished except in out memories. We can bring them alive again at another time, literally 're-member' them, if we all agree to or we can keep them alive just in our memories.

Drama as empowerment

Through dramatic play young children feel empowered! Being in role enables children safely to try out and experience what it might feel like to speak and act as someone else. It enables them to rehearse real life and what it feels like to be an adult and in control. Dramatic play lets children safely play out issues and past or future experiences that are disturbing or exciting them in real life and rehearse resolving them and taking control of them.

Drama as memory

Dramatic play and drama gives a special space for active reflection. While children are role-playing they are able to engage emotionally with the pretend and, even though they know the dramatic play or drama is not real life, the emotional connection with it is real. The connection between the emotions and drama makes it memorable. Any learning acquired through engagement with role is therefore also made memorable. Dramatic play, the drama lesson and the theatre are all important forums for personal, social and emotional development. The role-play area, the drama room and the stage are all significant spaces, full of infinite possibilities for memorable learning.

Drama as holistic education

As holistic child development, dramatic play is nature's gift. Drama and dramatic play involve engaging and developing the whole child (Figure 1.1).

What is 'drama in education' and 'drama for learning'?

Drama in Education (DiE) as it used to be called, or 'drama for learning' as it is more often called now, focuses primarily on creating shared make-believes to develop children's learning,

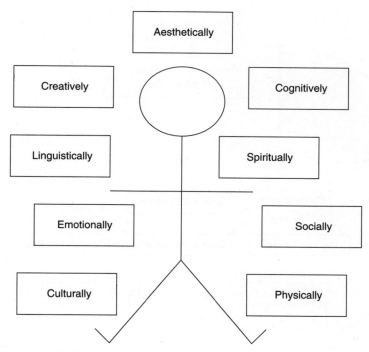

Figure 1.1 Drama engages and develops the whole child

confidence, self-esteem, creative and critical thinking, and communication skills through working in role (Figure 1.2). It may also be referred to as 'process drama' or, more recently, 'context drama'.

There are those who do drama under the wider umbrella of 'imaginative enquiry' and do not name it (or maybe not even recognize or acknowledge it) as drama. The burgeoning of circle time is interesting as it also has its roots in drama (being based on the socio-drama and psychodrama work of Jacob Moreno that has been adapted for schools by Jenny Mosely). You will note that many of the Drama Units use class circles on and off throughout. Also, the development of philosophy for children can be linked to drama as it encourages philosophical enquiry through the use of stories. All drama is story and is often used as a way of encouraging and developing philosophical thinking, frequently with the use of picture books that deal with big questions and issues.

Mantle of the Expert

There has been renewed interest in using 'Mantle of the Expert' (MoE) as an approach to learning and the more creative curriculum in some schools. 'Mantle of the Expert' was named by Dorothy Heathcote (Heathcote and Bolton, 1995), a highly influential and skilled drama practitioner and was a pioneering approach to teaching and learning in the 1960s and 1970s, which waned almost to extinction when the first content-laden National Curriculum was introduced and the Literacy and Numeracy Strategy Frameworks and Qualifications and Curriculum Authority (QCA) schemes of work arrived in schools.

'Mantle of the Expert' crosses curriculum boundaries (which is an approach now being encouraged again) and involves children engaging and working in role in a sustained way as experts with tasks to do. Again its roots are in dramatic play and drama, as children take on the roles of accomplished adults and become increasingly competent at related tasks. They rise to the occasion and are empowered by being treated as experts, with a resulting rise in self-esteem, confidence and

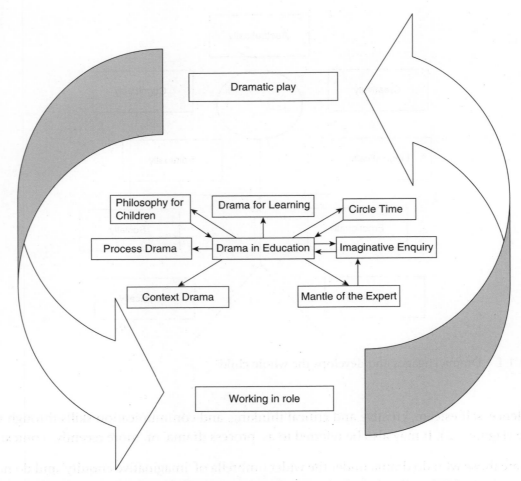

Figure 1.2 Current drama, story and role play linked learning initiatives and terminologies

skills. There is a taster of this to be found within Unit 5, when the children take on the role of expert designers of holiday developments working for an external client.

This resurgence of interest in MoE may be fuelled by the interest in methodologies that develop thinking skills and, more recently, the need to consider whether we are supporting children to develop entrepreneurship and thereby economic well-being.

To drama practitioners it is important that 'Mantle of the Expert' is acknowledged as drama and not just promoted as a curriculum approach or as enquiry-based learning. Many teachers using 'Mantle of the Expert' do not fully realize the drama heritage of 'Mantle of the Expert' and are missing a powerful opportunity to bring other drama strategies into play and extend further their teacher repertoire.

What drama skills do young children already have?

Young children who are developing normally come to school as experienced role players, already equipped with basic drama skills and powerful imaginations. If they are developing normally they can already pretend to be someone else (character), somewhere else (setting) and with something happening that is not really (plot). This is the essence of dramatic play, drama, story and theatre (Figure 1.3).

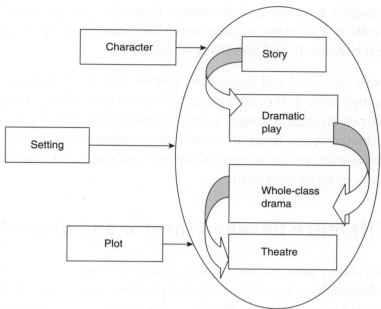

Figure 1.3 Narrative links

Since they were babies children have been able to imitate and mimic what they have observed in order to help them learn and they soon learn to re-enact scenarios rooted in what they have experienced and later create their own. The experiences they enact and re-enact may be from real life or from stories heard, seen or read.

Most young children will talk easily and naturally to imaginary creatures, animals and people, and sometimes keep the same important and necessary imaginary friends for as long as they need them, that is, for months or even years. Young children are also capable of imbuing inanimate objects with great emotional, sensory and symbolic significance, for example, the piece of blanket that a child needs to go to bed with. They also accept easily the notion that inanimate objects can have life, for example, accepting vehicles as characters in stories and films, and imagining their dolls and teddies are real companions that they can talk with. They readily engage with puppets and television characters as if they were real people. They can initiate and sustain chat based on make-believe with friends, relations and other adults who have not lost touch with the enjoyment and importance of 'pretend' to children and to themselves! Young children keenly serve pretend cups of tea and pieces of cake to those who are prepared to stay awhile to enter a make-believe with them. They will also spontaneously use 'ambiguous' objects as if they are something else, for example, a cardboard box as a spaceship, a blanketed clothes dryer as a tent, a bed as a boat! Objects are often used in this way in theatre as multi-purpose props, for example, Harlequin's stick. Put in theatre terms, young children create settings for their 'play', act out different characters and create plots, use simple objects and materials as props and sometimes as scenery, improvise dialogue and create scenes and short plays that are sometimes 'one offs' but are sometimes repeated.

How does drama link to story?

Story is important in the lives of children. All drama involves story, and drama lessons provide opportunity to create a shared living story that unfolds 'in the moment' at which it is happening.

Rehearsed theatre usually re-enacts and presents a story that already exists. In drama we are active, interactive, collective story-makers and storytellers who are living the story as we create it and engaging with it cognitively and affectively through role.

In every culture across the world and throughout history, humans make sense of the world and their place in it through story as they do through all the art forms. They may present their real-life or imagined stories through writings or enactments or sculptures or dances or music, for example. Through drama we can bring alive and enter existing stories to explore them together or we can create new stories. We can begin to know and understand the world, other people and our place and feelings in relation to both.

Is there a difference between theatre and drama?

Young children's own play or 'plays' are often repeated (almost ritualistically) and may almost become scripted as they are frequently replayed, for example, 'Let's play shopkeepers' or 'Let's play mums and dads', can to the initiated group of friends, involve demonstrating shared understandings about what will need to be said and done if you are allowed to join in. Dramatic play, like drama, can involve agreed rituals and will only work if all the participants follow the agreed rules of engagement. A maverick player, whether in the home corner or on the stage, jeopardizes the make-believe and is usually firmly dealt with by co-participants. Dramatic play is also very flexible and can be spontaneous and unrehearsed. Whether played or replayed, dramatic play is very engaging and motivational for young children. Dramatic play, drama and theatre can be seen as part of the same spectrum (or spiral) and it is best not to consider them as hierarchical with theatre as the icing on the cake (Figure 1.4).

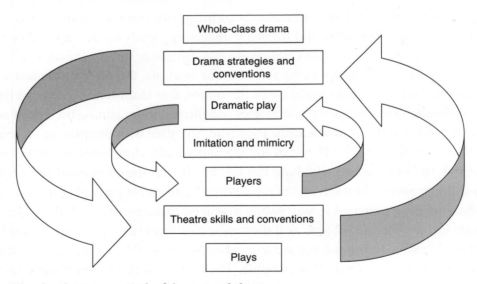

Figure 1.4   The development spiral of drama and theatre

Theatre is often devised and does not just rely on enacting play scripts written by playwrights and performing on stages. Theatre can happen anywhere (including classrooms) and can be arrived at by consensus, from a reworking of scenes that have first been improvised. Within drama lessons we may well devise short pieces of theatre for each other as part of the drama, to help us communicate our understandings in an aesthetic way to ourselves and our fellow participants. When we know the human-made boundaries of conventional theatre we can deliberately play with them in effective and playful ways. Some forms of theatre invite the audience not just to observe but to interact verbally or even physically with the performance and participate in various ways, for example, Forum Theatre and Pantomime.

Dramatic play skills are also drama skills. Theatre, like dramatic play, is about people pretending to be someone else, somewhere else with something happening that is not really. But theatre usually implies that we prepare this sustained make-believe or 'play' for an external audience and not just for ourselves. We aim to help an audience to experience, understand and be affected by a play.

Who should be teaching the drama?

Artsmark (an Arts Council England initiative that recognizes different levels of good arts provision in schools – www.artsmark.org.uk) has been very successful at getting drama in its own right onto the timetable of an ever-increasing number of schools. To get basic Artsmark, drama needs to be given its own regular, timetabled slot. However, many schools put drama on the timetable to get Artsmark but then are unsure about what to do developmentally in a regular drama lesson. If they do not understand the depth and breadth of what drama in schools can be and there are no drama specialist teachers to support drama teaching in the school, then the slot may be used narrowly or repetitively.

It is important that at a time when structures are being put in place to enable drama specialist teachers from Specialist Arts Colleges and secondary Advanced Skills Teachers and theatre educators to work in primary schools, that the primary drama slot is not simply handed over by primary teachers to others who may not necessarily have a professional understanding of young children's learning and all-round development or of the Primary Curriculum or of whole-class drama. This could hamper the integration of drama as pedagogy across the primary curriculum and its integration and development in and across the creative curriculum.

We must ensure that teachers and teaching assistants understand the place of drama across the curriculum and are competent at it so that drama does not become an 'add on' provided by others and that there is not an overemphasis on scripted performance and plays.

It is also important that drama does not just happen in the Extended School slot where it is not necessarily accessed by all children and may be detached from the core educational experiences and entitlement of all children. We should be open to working with creative partners in drama, but recognize what experienced primary practitioners can and must bring to a real drama/ theatre for learning partnership. We still need to develop drama practitioners who are rooted in schools and child development and are not just visitors who are focused only on plays and theatre skills, with no sustained connection with the school and the children's learning.

Who should lead and manage drama in the school?

Few head teachers are themselves drama specialists, even when they are English specialists. All teachers should have an understanding of teaching in and through drama, and with the enhanced role of teaching assistants it is necessary that they too become proficient at using its methodology and maybe teaching drama. All schools need someone to lead and manage drama just as they do any other curriculum area. If drama is to be an important part of the methodology and pedagogical toolbox of all teachers and teaching assistants, then the leadership and management of the school have a responsibility to arrange leadership and professional development for their staff in this area, and not just skirt around the issue by passing drama over to external providers or ignoring drama altogether. Drama is a core and statutory entitlement at present as part of English, so all primary children must receive it.

Through becoming skilled at teaching in and through drama, we can support whole classes of children to imagine they are anyone, anywhere, at any point in time, in any place and in any situation. What an infinitely flexible teaching medium drama is and one that every teacher can benefit from.

Through the units of drama work in this book alone we can meet and interact with Samuel Pepys and Howard Carter in history, enter the tomb of Tutankhamun, challenge land developers in geography, talk with and advise migrants in personal and social education (PSE), as well as explore an underwater world and help a bullied mermaid. We can meet characters in poems and a painter as we escape the Fire of London as well as defeat a Samurai Warrior. Why would we want to develop the drama teaching skills of only one member of staff when we can use drama as an enjoyable and infinitely flexible methodology right across the curriculum?

How can I get support to teach drama?

It makes a difference if teachers and assistants experience being in drama themselves as participants with other teachers as well as with their own class as co-participants. Accessing drama in-service training (INSET) and continuing professional development (CPD) with a practical element is advisable as we all know that reading about something is not a substitute for experiencing it. If you are asking children to do drama, then having fairly recently experienced what it feels like yourself to be in role with others is beneficial. Some local authorities provide drama courses with strong practical elements for teachers, as do subject associations (www.nationaldrama.co.uk) and several commercial companies.

There is an increase in the numbers of freelance drama consultants and theatre educators available to work in schools. Find out a little about exactly what they are offering as some may be helping you with staging performances, while others are teaching about whole-class process drama as pedagogy. It is worth asking where they have recently worked and taking the time to phone or email to get a first-hand evaluation. Also, of course, they must be police checked if they are working in your school.

There are also companies and consultants that teach predominantly about a particular aspect of drama for learning, for example, MoE (www.mantleoftheexpert.com). It is best to explore MoE once you have already acquired some broader drama training. However, there may be teachers whose interest in drama for learning generally has been kindled through specific learning about MoE. Teachers whose introduction to drama is initially through MoE only may acquire some alternative, parallel drama convention vocabularies.

Some local authorities have drama advisers (but not many) or arts advisers who might put you in touch with advice and support. Often drama advice nowadays comes from National Strategy consultants as part of their work in schools linked to developing speaking and listening rather than to drama as an art form.

Drama and the Curriculum

Where is drama in the curriculum?

Drama in England is currently placed within English, which many specialist drama practitioners find difficult to accept. Many English teachers who are unsure about how to teach drama themselves also find drama in English problematic as they may not have been drama trained and yet are English teachers.

It is important not to ignore the non-verbal and non-scripted aspects of drama. Drama is an ancient, multi-sensory, aesthetic and cultural art form which integrates sound, image and movement and involves the interaction of both verbal and non-verbal communication to make and communicate meanings. Drama being placed within English has led to a very literacy-focused type of drama happening in most schools, where drama is often used mainly to improve speaking and listening and writing. Drama is a great way to teach English and can improve writing, speaking and listening (Figure 2.1), but it needs to be seen as more than a tool for the development of other strands of English. Drama is a great pedagogy but is not just there to service other subjects.

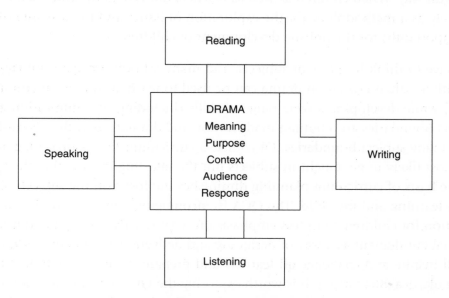

Figure 2.1 Drama can integrate reading, writing, speaking and listening

Drama offers English a great deal. It potentially provides an endless range of imagined audiences for speaking and listening and an endless range of imagined contexts for creating different genres of writing for different purposes. It also, of course, links directly with play scripts, which will hopefully have been devised or brought alive initially through drama, rather than approached as just a decontextualized writing task. If children are scriptwriting it is important that the scripts are brought alive through drama and they actively experience the connection. It also may be that what has been improvised in drama can then be scripted afterwards.

All drama is story, and story can be brought alive, created, explored and developed through drama. We can co-operatively create, become, meet, question and develop characters. With young children this may be supported through dramatic small-world play or speaking through puppets. We can actively devise, explore, extend and elaborate plots together. We can have access to the teacher or teaching assistant in role, modelling different types of speech for different purposes and audiences.

Where else could drama be in your curriculum, now and in the future?

Drama can be used in any curriculum area and embedded across the curriculum, but it is important that drama also is taught in its own right in order to embed and use it well elsewhere. To use drama well teachers and teaching assistants need to know what drama is and how to actually do it. No one would expect teachers to be able to embed and use information and communication technology (ICT) across the curriculum without learning about ICT and acquiring some ICT skills themselves first (preferably practically) and then learning how best to teach it. The same holds true for drama.

Drama in the primary school needs to be about developing children as rounded people through role play and working in role *as well as* about developing their drama and theatre skills. Drama should therefore be taught separately as well as within a range of lessons, in order for children to get better at drama itself and to acquire and develop drama and theatre skills in a systematic and meaningful way. When children as well as teachers understand drama, then it can be used most effectively as a methodology for the exploration of issues and the teaching of all subjects and, most importantly, for the holistic development of children.

We do not have to think in terms of subjects, and many schools are again moving away from doing so. With a little imagination drama can be used to teach absolutely anything in any curriculum area, while developing a wide range of skills (including communication and thinking skills). Subject boundaries are a human-made notion and dramatic play flows seamlessly across, and merges, many subject boundaries. Of course, a curriculum that is presented as subjects to teachers is most likely to get taught in subjects but the new 'Big Picture' that the QCA are presenting as the basis of curriculum planning diminishes the focus on the subjects and enhances the focus on learning and the child. The QCA is encouraging a move towards a more process-based education for children, with less emphasis on what exactly is taught and more emphasis on experiential entitlement as a way of designing and delivering a 'modern world class curriculum that will inspire and challenge all learners and prepare them for the future' (QCA, 2007, www.qca.org.uk./qca_8644.aspx). It is worth exploring the QCA website, and not just reading a hardback copy of the National Curriculum, as this will help teachers approach the curriculum through different filters and lenses and more flexibly (www.qca.org.uk).

DRAMA AND THE CURRICULUM

Although there is less emphasis again now on separate subjects in primary schools (with the inevitable exception usually of subjects in which children still sit Standard Assessment Tests SATs) and Tasks there is a convincing case to be made for drama being made a subject in its own right. This is unlikely to happen at a time when subject content is being slimmed down. Nonetheless, schools can and should teach both in and through drama.

With a renewed emphasis on thematic, cross-curricular, process and skills-based rather than content-based teaching (as encouraged through *Excellence and Enjoyment*, DfES, 2003a) and through the QCA 'Big Picture', drama is important as a process-based, cross-curricular teaching approach with its own set of skills and accessible methodology. It seems likely that drama will not receive subject status in the next revised curriculum but that its place as a pedagogy may be secured and strengthened.

Research evidence shows that drama is most frequently used within primary schools within English, religious education, history, and personal, social and emotional education (Downing et al., 2003).

Drama is used to:

- explore current issues, for example, environmental sustainability (Unit 5)

- understand the motivations of people from other times, for example, archaeologists investigating ancient Egypt (Unit 6) and diarists (Unit 3)

- gain insight into the lives of people in other places, times and cultures, for example, migrants (Unit 7) seventeenth-century Londoners (Unit 3)

- explore alternative viewpoints, for example, residents, property developers and environmentalists (Unit 5)

- consider the impact of human actions on places, for example, the entering of Tutankhamun's tomb (Unit 6)

- consider the impact of actions on other people, for example, bullying (Unit 2)

- empower children through enabling them to see that they are agents of change, for example, they can work together to have an impact on bullying (Unit 2)

- enable children to gain a sense of themselves as cultural beings, who can identify with, make and respond to culture/s (Unit 4)

- stimulate curiosity and enquiry by the children, for example, finding out more about what protected species need (Unit 5), discovering what firefighting methods were available in seventeenth-century London (Unit 3), finding out about various waves of migration (Unit 7), and so on.

What about assessment of drama?

With drama being placed as a strand of speaking and listening within English, clearly its summative assessment should contribute to levels of attainment in speaking and listening and English. These assessments tell us what a child was able to attain at a particular point in time.

However, no programme of study exists nationally for drama and no statutory National Curriculum levels for drama have been produced by the Qualifications and Curriculum Authority. However the renewed National Strategy Frameworks do offer end-of-year objectives and the Early Learning Goals for the Foundation Stage offer an end-of-year objective.

The renewed Primary National Strategy Framework for literacy (DfES, 2006)

www.standards.dfes.gov.uk/primaryframework/downloads/PDF/PF_Literacy_by_year_alt.pdf

All children at Key Stages 1, 2 and 3 must have drama as part of the statutory National Curriculum for English.

From September 2007 primary schools are expected to be working with the renewed Primary National Strategy Framework for literacy. This includes the following drama strand as part of the core learning:

Core learning in literacy

Speak and listen for a wide range of purposes in different contexts

Drama strand

Most children learn to:

- use dramatic techniques including working in role to explore ideas and texts
- create, share and evaluate ideas through drama

Foundation Stage

- Use language to recreate roles and experiences (Early Learning Goal)

Year 1

- Explore familiar themes and characters through improvisation and role-play
- Act out their own and well-known stories, using voices for characters
- Discuss why they like a performance

Year 2

- Adopt appropriate roles in small or large groups and consider alternative courses of action
- Present part of traditional stories, their own stories or work drawn from different parts of the curriculum for members of their own class
- Consider how mood and atmosphere are created in live or recorded performance

Year 3

- Present events and characters through dialogue to engage the interest of an audience
- Use some drama strategies to explore stories or issues
- Identify and discuss qualities of others' performances, including gesture, action and costume

Year 4

- Create roles showing how behaviour can be interpreted from different viewpoints
- Develop scripts based improvisation
- Comment constructively on plays and performances, discussing effects and how they are achieved

Year 5

- Reflect upon how working in role helps to explore complex issues
- Perform a scripted scene making use of dramatic conventions
- Use and recognise the impact of theatrical effects in drama

Year 6

- Improvise using a range of drama strategies and conventions to explore such themes as hopes, fears and desires
- Consider the overall impact of a live or recorded performance, identifying dramatic ways of conveying characters' ideas and building tension
- Devise a performance considering how to adapt the performance for a specific audience

Year 6 progression into Year 7

- Develop drama techniques to explore in role a variety of situations and texts or respond to stimuli
- Develop drama techniques and strategies anticipating, visualising and problem solving in different learning contexts
- Work collaboratively to devise and present scripted and unscripted pieces that maintain the attention of an audience, and reflect on and evaluate their own presentations and those of others. (DfES, 2006, www.standards.dfes.gov.uk/primaryframework/downloads/ PDF/PF_Literacy_by_year_alt. pdf)

If you track across the literacy strands other than drama, you will find that through drama you can also link to some of the requirements of other strands, that is, reading, writing, group interaction and discussion, as well as those within other curriculum areas.

Arts Council England level descriptors for drama

Arts Council England (ACE) have published a cross-phase document to support the teaching of drama in schools, entitled *Drama in Schools: Second Edition* (ACE, 2002). The first edition was published just after the National Curriculum was introduced, when drama did not receive discrete subject status. The second edition has been much revised and contains a poster of a set of level descriptors for drama that some schools may find useful when planning for continuity and progression. This is also available via the Arts Council England website (www.artscouncil.org.uk). There are eight levels presented, followed by an 'Exceptional performance' level. However, these are not statutory levels and there may be a significant element of subjectivity in applying them. Many schools remain unaware these unofficial levels exist. They are intended primarily to support continuity and progression rather than formal, summative assessment. In the absence of anything else of significance, schools sometimes use them but this is more often secondary schools where the management demand to level drama is stronger.

The ACE levels can optionally be used alongside the National Primary Strategy materials for speaking and listening that are part of the renewed framework. This lack of a discrete drama curriculum from the QCA with a programme of study and associated levels is not very helpful to schools in terms of planning drama confidently for continuity and progression. Schools will find they need to work with several publications to hand when planning their own drama curriculum.

The Arts Council levels focus on drama in three interrelated ways: Making, Performing and Responding.

Making (or creating) encompasses the many processes and activities employed when exploring, devising, shaping and interpreting drama. It can involve working alone and with others to create drama.

Performing covers the skills and knowledge displayed when enacting, presenting and producing dramas. The performance may involve enacting to and with your classmates and not necessarily to an external audience. In drama lessons the children are actors and also spectators.

Responding involves reflecting on emotional and intellectual reactions to the drama. This may be through a spoken or written response or through a response through drama itself. Responses may be individual and personal or can be group or whole-class responses. They can respond to aspects of the drama, for example, content, form, character, language, gesture, and so on. (Arts Council England, 2002: 29)

The Arts Council levels provide specific criteria for each of the eight levels and for exceptional performance. Remember that the levels are not statutory or arrived at through the usual official processes but, nonetheless, can be a useful guide. The levels have maybe a stronger theatre emphasis than a 'process drama' emphasis and schools will need to decide their own balance if they decide to use ACE levels as well as National Curriculum Speaking and Listening levels (which are formal levels). There is an expectation in National Curriculum subject assessments that children should reach at least level 2 by the end of Key Stage (KS) 1 and Level 4 by the end of KS2. The Arts Council-suggested level criteria for these levels are the following:

Level	Making	Performing	Responding
2	Pupils can: • Take part in a range of drama activities and use simple theatre devices/techniques, for example, narration and still image • Explore problems in an imagined world and make up plays from stories and other stimuli • Use the dialogue in existing texts as well as create their own	Pupils can: • Prepare and learn a few lines in their plays • Add simple theatrical effects such as sound effect or significant prop to enhance the work they perform to others • Use their voices and their bodies to create characters and atmospheres, employing language appropriate to the role or character, for example, adopting a more formal tone when the situation requires it	Pupils can: • Recognise different kinds of dramas, for example, a TV 'soap' and their own fantasy play • Explain in simple terms how atmosphere is created in plays • Talk about why they made certain decisions in their play and discuss how their work and that of others could be improved by more practice or better staging • Make simple connections between the dramas they experience and their own lives
4	Pupils can: • Work confidently in groups using a range of drama techniques to explore situations and devise drama for different purposes • Plan and structure plays that make use of a range of techniques and forms to express their ideas, for example, narration in story theatre, mask work, mime, physical theatre • Actively interpret the work of playwrights • Write and perform their own simple scripts, demonstrating an understanding of some correct theatre conventions • Establish a character, with control over movement and voice	Pupils can: • Select and operate a range of simple theatre technologies to create the right space for their drama and to enhance their work • Learn lines, collaborate with others and organise simple presentations • Experiment with their voices and movement, to create or present different characters in performance	Pupils can: • Demonstrate an awareness of some theatre traditions from different times and places, for example, Kathakali dance drama, Greek and Tudor theatre • Discuss the themes or issues in drama and the way they were presented • Reflect on and evaluate their own and other people's work, suggest improvements and use correct basic theatre terminology • Comment on how intended effects have been achieved, for example, the use of silence

Source: *Drama in Schools* (2002) 32: 5, Arts Council England. www.artscouncil.org.uk/documents/publications/725.pdf

Formative assessment or assessment for learning, however, is ongoing and builds directly on what a child can do and, most importantly, focuses on what they need to do next in order to improve. The teacher may be assessing the drama product but, as important, is assessing the drama process. As with assessment for learning in other subject areas, it is important that the child is part of the assessment process and knows what is expected of them and what they need to do to achieve next steps and improve participation and outcome. In drama, with the teacher as both assessor and a co-participant in the drama process, it is possible to assess while the teacher is in role as well as out of role. What a teacher sees children are achieving in the drama lesson should inform adjustments in the teaching. In drama the choice of next teacher move and the selection of the next drama strategy or convention should be in part influenced by how the children are already performing and responding. Clearly, for teachers and teaching assistants new to teaching drama it is acceptable and understandable that they will follow a pre-planned lesson more rigidly but, as confidence grows, the teacher becomes more able to adjust the drama teaching at the time, to the benefit of the children's learning and the drama.

Expectations need to be clear and shared if you are assessing against specific criteria. If you are working with a freeze frame, you might want to state clearly what you are expecting to see in relation to the form or content, for example, 'I want you to be sure that you all move into the freeze-frame in slow motion, that you all freeze at the same moment and that you hold it totally still for five seconds'. The performance success criteria are clear and the children can match each other's performances against the criteria. You might say, 'Each character will then speak one line only. You will repeat the short scene twice but the second time the characters will say the line differently and I want those watching to tell me what difference it makes'. 'What advice would you give to the actors in this scene when they play it again? What worked well and what might they change to make this scene even clearer?'

What about assessment through drama?

As well as assessing the progress children are making in drama (which many schools are not doing), drama is sometimes used as a way of assessing other areas. For example the drama 'Billy's Bucket' (Unit 2) can be used to assess whether or not children have learned practical approaches that can be used to deal with bullying. Also, when creating a drama based on a historical event such as 'The Discovery of the Tomb of Tutankhamun' (Unit 6), the children will be revealing their current knowledge and understanding of, for example, the ancient Egyptians during the lesson and within the drama they create. When children are making or creating drama and when they are working and responding in role they are usually speaking and listening. Again this is an assessment opportunity. Some teachers deliberately set up drama situations to assess particular types of speech being used for particular purposes. In 'Billy's Bucket', for example, the children are required to use persuasive speech when they try to persuade Billy to have a birthday present other than a bucket. They are required to use descriptive speech when they describe themselves as buckets. They use instructional speech when they advise the mermaid how to deal with the Bully Fish, and so on. The children's responses can contribute evidence for assessment of their social, personal and emotional skills. With a little preparation drama is a very good forum for assessing many aspects of learning. It helps to have a second adult present when assessing, as being the drama teacher and recording assessments simultaneously can be difficult. Of course, the use of filming can help here and can provide a useful record.

How does drama link to Every Child Matters?

The British government has stated aims for every child. These are that they will be supported to:

- be healthy
- stay safe
- enjoy and achieve
- make a positive contribution
- achieve economic well-being.

Drama and theatre have much to offer children in relation to the pursuit of all these outcomes.

Be healthy

With regard to children's health and well-being, the therapeutic links between the arts and mental health are evident within psychodrama and socio-drama. Drama enables psychological and social issues to be expressed, opened up and dealt with in a safe and distanced way through the use of play and replay in role. However, psychodrama and socio-drama are specialist domains and should not intentionally be entered into by mainstream drama teachers in schools. Drama in schools does sometimes make evident to adults problems that children are dealing with. It can then offer a supportive and safe space in which cognitive shifts can occur.

Drama involves physical movement and some forms of drama and theatre, for example, physical theatre, can be quite physically demanding and contribute to physical health.

Drama can be focused to specifically present and open up health and safety issues and educate them about, for example, bullying or healthy eating. With older children drama is often used as a means of opening up and dealing with issues relating to sexual health and drug misuse. In drama children can practise how to say 'no' in a range of situations and consider the outcomes of different courses of action.

Stay safe

The well-managed drama lesson is a safe, social space. Children are protected and supported by the group. Operating in role safely distances children.

Drama lessons can be used as a forum for dealing with specific issues to do with safety and the prevention of accidents. Although the children are working in a fiction, they can be dealing with realistic safety issues and the learning can be made explicit and transferable to outside the drama lesson.

Enjoy and achieve

Enjoyment is the key word that comes up again and again when you talk with children (or adults) about their feelings about drama. Children would not spend so long pretending and role-playing in imagined worlds, voluntarily, out of school if they did not find pretending enjoyable. If you ask adults to recall their feelings when they played 'make-believe' as a child, most will include the word 'enjoyed' in their response (Baldwin, 2004).

In make-believe worlds, what children can imagine they are achieving is limitless and the feeling of success a child gets through succeeding in role can stay with them beyond the drama and into real life.

What children actually can achieve and attain through drama is wide-ranging and includes:

- a sense of group and class belonging

- success in creating collaboratively (process and product)

- a sense of shared ownership

- a listening and responsive audience

- an awareness of being able to impact on the thoughts and ideas of others

- friendship and co-operation with peers

- greater understanding of oneself (attitudes, beliefs, feelings)

- raised awareness of one's social and cultural place in relation to others

- increased subject knowledge acquired memorably

- success in working towards the same goal as part of a team (negotiation, perseverance, compromise)

- enjoyment and a sense of satisfaction.

Make a positive contribution

Because drama is a social activity, it relies for its success on everyone's positive contributions to keep the make-believe and the drama process going. When contributions are made and accepted, it is within the context of immediate whole-class feedback and approval. Individual contributions become accepted into the collective drama and this raises the self-esteem of the child who contributes. Children's ideas are used and developed in drama in education. It is not just about enacting drama activity that is being directed by the teacher or director.

When children are involved in drama performance they realize that everyone's positive contribution is vital to the overall success of the performance.

Achieve economic well-being

When children are involved in creating successful drama performance, either in drama lessons or as theatre for audiences, the individual and team skills used and developed are considerable and of the type valued by employers. The skills that are developed in drama lessons are life skills and not just drama skills. They are the sort of 'people skills' necessary in life and in the workplace, for example, critical and creative thinking, good communication, understanding people's verbal and non-verbal signals, making clear presentations, teamwork, perseverance, and so on. Drama in education is preparation for life.

The creative industries are the fastest growing employment area, and developing creative thinking through drama can not only set children on the path to working in the theatre or related industries but can equip them to think creatively within any chosen career that will support their economic well-being. Many careers of the future have not yet been imagined. Creative thinking and adaptability will be absolutely necessary for our children as future employees and drama enables and develops this.

Drama Publications

Which recent documents and official publications can help me to teach drama?

Ironically it was not long after drama became part of the compulsory National Curriculum for English (within the speaking and listening strand) that the original National Literacy Strategy arrived in schools. For several years the Literacy Strategy had no speaking and listening strand. The National Literacy Strategy effectively became the English Curriculum, despite the fact that it was originally focused only on reading and writing. In time the speaking and listening strands were added in, first as a supplementary booklet and later as part of the National Strategy Framework. Speaking and listening is, after all, the cornerstone of English.

Some useful basic drama materials have been published by the National Primary Strategy at various times.

Speaking, Listening, Learning: Working with Children at Key Stages 1 and 2 (DfES, 2004)

These materials (within a plastic box distributed to all schools) are very much focused on the development of speaking and listening using drama methodology rather than the development of drama itself. However, they contain short explanations of some basic drama strategies that are now in place in many schools within literacy lessons, for example, freeze-frame, thought tracking and hot-seating, but did not highlight 'teacher in role,' which is the most powerful strategy of all.

The materials do give a short explanation of 'Forum Theatre', which arguably would benefit from more detailed information to support teachers in its use. Forum Theatre is fascinating, versatile and follows a set of rules that enable the audience to become not just spectators but directors and actors (spect-actors) when a performance is replayed. This approach is based on the work of Augusto Boal (2002) and is an important approach to personal and social change through enactment and re-enactment. The audience watch a short, prepared performance once and then have the right to intervene and direct in agreed ways when the play is repeated, for example, asking an actor to respond differently at a key moment and then considering what the effect of this change has on other characters and outcomes. The aim is to effect desirable change for the characters and in doing so learn how consciously responding differently can empower characters (and us, in real life) to effect change.

The National Primary Strategy speaking and listening materials also omit 'Mantle of the Expert' which is an important and long-established drama approach to learning and enquiry across the curriculum.

Drama Objectives Bank (DfES, 2003b)

This was produced by the National Secondary Strategy and is useful to primary schools also. The book contained good explanations of the main drama strategies and conventions that can be used in both phases. It may be worth asking your local high school if you can see their copy or maybe they have a spare one. It is now out of print but can be downloaded at www.standards. dfes.gov.uk/secondary/keystage3/all/respub/en_dramaobjs

Creativity: Find it! Promote it!

The QCA completed a three-year project (commencing 2000) on teaching for creativity across the curriculum. It was called 'Creativity: Find it! Promote it!' and it has resulted in the gathering and web publication of many lessons that are judged to be good examples of creative teaching of the national curriculum. A very high proportion of these lessons involve the use of role play and drama both in and beyond English. This resource bank of lessons is available at www.ncaction.co.uk.

Drama for Learning and Creativity (D4LC)

An initiative that has received the national support of the QCA is D4LC. It started as a partnership project between the subject association National Drama (www.nationaldrama.co.uk) and a local authority (Norfolk) in 2005, and initially involved drama specialists working alongside 120 teachers in schools of all types and phases, to improve teaching for creativity and raise standards through the use of drama. Teachers contribute best practice lesson examples and these are posted free of charge to all teachers on the website (www.d4lc.org). The full and very positive evaluation of this successful initiative can also be read there. The associated publication which contains edited lessons for Primary and Secondary teachers (NCC and ND, 2007) can be ordered online. The author of this book is the national Director of D4LC.

What drama books and other resources can help me plan and teach drama?

There are now quite a few teaching books on the market for drama in schools. Different types of drama book are likely to appeal to different teachers and teaching assistants. Which books suit you best may well depend on your level of experience and personal preference. Beware those that just shower you with drama activities without providing any rationale for doing them! You will get to the end of the book and if you do not know or understand the thinking behind the activities you will be less able and less likely to develop your own high-quality drama. The ideas within such drama books may be perfectly good ideas, but select from them within the context of a planned drama framework and make sure that if you use this sort of book you make the connections that are missing. *Ask yourself why you are choosing a particular activity and what you expect it to help the children to achieve or improve at?* If you do not know, then why do it? Lots of drama activities and drama games can be fun, social and enjoyable, some may develop drama skills, but without a framework the activities do not help you develop a sustained and meaningful drama that leads to learning, continuity and progression.

There are also books that give you fairly detailed theory about drama and education with examples of practice thinly threaded through. Often abstracting the lesson from these books in a usable way can be difficult, especially for those with little drama experience. This type of drama book is more useful to fairly experienced teachers of drama who want to gain a deeper understanding of the drama process. They are not necessarily the books that help you plan a curriculum but may help you to articulate to yourself and others why drama is important and what it can achieve. They help you gain a vision of what drama is about but may not give you actual clear lessons to pick up and try.

There are also books that offer theory and practice in linked yet practically accessible ways. These tend to have a theoretical underpinning that is not too detailed and yet also provide separately lessons and units of work that exemplify the theory in practice. You are offered complete lessons but, hopefully, you will be told and will know why you are doing them, and this supports you in developing your own. Or maybe busy teachers and assistants just grab the lessons and do not read the theory but can sense that they offer progression and fit into what they are trying to achieve. There is a recommended reading list at the end of this book.

What about BBC Radio drama programmes for schools?

These offer some progression between series and link well to the National Curriculum and parts of the national strategies. They use many established and well-proven drama strategies and conventions, including teacher in role. Teachers and teaching assistants are well supported throughout the programmes (as are the children) and they may particularly suit those who are not yet secure about leading the drama lesson. It is better to use a good recorded drama programme rather than deny children drama. It is probably best to have recordings of the programmes (which can be purchased) and slot the units into the appropriate curriculum time and place, rather than follow them in a linear way.

Teachers and teaching assistants might start out using the BBC programmes but, hopefully, will increasingly turn them off and experiment, developing parts of the drama themselves and maybe in time leading the whole drama. Start to kick away the support and take ownership yourself. You can always return to the security of the recording if necessary, but be brave and push your own boundaries and comfort zone! A teacher or teaching assistant should ideally listen to the programme first anyway and, having heard the programme, may feel confident enough to lead the drama without using the recording.

Experienced drama teachers still sometimes turn to these programme themes and teachers notes as a resource bank and use them as a stimulus from which to develop their own dramas. If you are looking for children's picture books that are suitable for exploration through drama, then the Key Stage 1 drama programmes that are based on stories, for example, *Let's Make a Story*, are a secure starting point. *First Steps in Drama* and *Drama Workshop* will also support your cross-curricular drama work, www.bbc.co.uk/schoolradio/drama.

How do I choose picture books and stories for drama?

A picture book or story can offer the framework for a drama lesson (Unit 2). All drama is story and some good stories have been published in very visual ways. You will be using them to stimulate drama and new scenes that are not already in the book, rather than just acting out what the book has in it. Good picture books deal with big questions and issues that often can be opened up and explored through drama (Unit 7).

There are no hard and fast rules about how to select picture books for drama, but those that have a community under threat will immediately provide parts for everyone and dramatic tension. Problems to be solved by or for characters give an imperative for thought and action. Of course, you can create characters and problems to be solved through drama that are not in the book at all; for example, Simon's brother in Unit 7 does not exist in the book and there is no mermaid that has been bullied in the book on which Unit 2 is based. Books that involve a journey that needs to be made, or a discovery, are also easy to use for drama, as there is an immediate purposeful activity to build on. If the journey or discovery is not actually in a book, you can always put it in; for example, Billy does not really go inside the bucket in the picture book that Unit 2 is based on but, of course, in the drama he does.

A good book illustration can be a powerful stand-alone drama stimulus. The work of Shaun Tan, Chris van Allsburg, Chris Waddell, Anthony Browne and Chris Pepper are all worth exploring with an eye to using them as a stimulus for drama. Most illustrators have websites that are well worth a visit.

Narrative poetry for drama

Narrative poetry is story and so again is good as source material for drama. Poems are not usually as long as books, so they can be more manageable and easier to access and explore thoroughly through drama. Narrative poetry is a requirement for study in the National Primary Strategy and drama can make it an active and memorable learning experience (Unit 8). You can use the methodology contained in Unit 8 to approach other narrative poems, for example, ' The Lady of Shallot', 'Flannan Isle', 'The Highwayman', 'The Jabberwocky'. All can be found via the Internet.

What can the Internet and World Wide Web offer my drama teaching?

It is easy to see how the Internet can be used to support secondary examination syllabuses and theatre education through access to plays and playwrights. It is still emerging as a way of supporting process drama in education, which involves socially working in role as a group and takes place face to face and 'in the moment'. What is important is to make sure that the drama itself drives the direction of the drama lessons, not the technology, which is just a tool that should support the drama itself rather than shape it.

The Internet can also offer direct access to the services of the main subject association for drama educators, National Drama (www.nationaldrama.co.uk) and their membership forums. The Internet has several established drama e-groups that enable people teaching drama to support each other and share ideas, for example, the D4LC website (www.d4lc.org), the Mantle of the Expert website (www.mantleoftheexpert.com) and Ken Taylor's Drama UK website (mainly secondary) (www.kentaylor.co.uk), to name but a few. International drama websites, such as www.dramatool.org and www.idea-org.net, are also worth visiting to get a global dimension and understanding of drama for learning. Curriculum Online (www.curriculumonline.gov.uk) has some drama exemplars under speaking and listening in English.

National Drama is developing online Continuing Professional Development materials for the Teacher Development Agency. The whole World Wide Web offers access to an enormous source of images and text that can stimulate and support drama, including historical photographs and authentic historical documents and texts, music and poetry sites, paintings and sculptures, music and sound effects, and artists' and illustrators' websites.

It is worth gathering a whole range of resources around any theme you are teaching through drama, and drama teachers are always on the hunt for stimuli, much of which can be found via the Internet. Care must of course be taken to ensure that any copyright is taken account of.

CHAPTER 4

A Time and Place for Drama

Do I need the hall or a special drama space to do drama in?

You may wish to define a specific space as the drama space but this is up to you. Particularly with young children there may be a space that becomes 'the drama space'. It may be just a few large physical education (PE) mats put together or an area defined by floor markings or a carpet that can become the space we meet in or on, so that we can all enter a pretend world. Just gathering in a seated 'drama circle' can be the signal that we are about to start a drama lesson and enter a make-believe together.

If your school is lucky enough to have a drama studio then you already have a defined space for make believe as well as a public acceptance that drama is important and warrants its own space. It does not mean that you cannot also do drama in the classroom or out of doors. The lack of a hall or studio should never be a reason for not providing children with drama. Drama is working in role and, if necessary, it is possible (but not ideal) to be in role sat at your classroom desks. If you never moved drama from sitting at desks on chairs, then the options for dramatic strategies would be physically very limited, but it is up to the adult taking the lesson to creatively adapt the situation and environment to enable drama. When drama is defined as being in role together, rather than necessarily performing plays, it can happen in any space. It depends what you are going to be physically doing in a drama lesson as to where you need to be space-wise.

There are pros and cons associated with moving into a different space as a drama space. It shifts children's expectations about the activity that is about to happen. It shifts the way children think about lessons when they move into different working environments in preparation for them. However, if the drama you will be doing is quite static and confined to a small space for some reason, then the hall may not be as suitable as the classroom. Young children particularly can become too lost in large spaces if they mostly work in the classroom, and sometimes a smaller drama space is more suitable and less intimidating to start with. Sometimes young children think that because they are in the hall then it must be PE and may try to dash about if you do not make expectations about drama lesson behaviours clear.

If you are using drama frequently as a methodology across the curriculum, then you will probably not be able to or want to use the hall each time you are doing drama. If you are using the hall, then make the space work to the advantage of the drama. You can tailor the drama strategies used to suit larger or smaller spaces as necessary, for example, hot-seating lends itself to a restricted space more easily than a 'Conscience Alley' that requires all children to stand in two long lines facing each other. Hot-seating does not require much more than a chair, and the rest of the class could be seated at their desks if necessary. Freeze-frames by definition are static and can be done in classrooms. Be aware that if drama mostly happens in the classroom then you are probably being consistently restrictive in the way you are working and you may be overusing more physically static strategies. Make sure that you sometimes get into the hall if you can (or out of doors if you have no hall) and work in a larger space that enables more physical movement and greater physical separation between groups working.

What about doing drama outdoors?

It has already been said that drama can happen anywhere. Just watch children in the playground and on the school field and often you will see dramatic play going on spontaneously out of doors. The outdoors naturally inspires dramatic play, stimulates the imagination and gives physical freedom. It is interestingly often the type of primitive survival play that involves running and building pretend shelters and being chased and hunted … and, unfortunately, 'pretend' fighting. It is often superhero play imitating the heroes portrayed by the media. It used to be cowboys and Indians years ago and now it is computer game characters.

Sometimes the out-of-doors learning environment will lend itself to particular dramas and can stimulate and enhance them. Many schools have outdoor structures or natural spaces in their grounds that lend themselves to dramatic activity and drama. For example, a willow dome or tunnel can be an exciting space to use as part of a drama setting, as can a clump of bushes or a copse of trees. Also (with due attention to health and safety) there may be climbing structures and outdoor play equipment that can be used within dramas for particular purposes. However, do not let equipment get in the way of the drama. If it proves to be distracting or restricting, then it is better to imagine the props and drama environment than use real play equipment and structures that can distract or over-dominate the direction of the drama.

Off-site drama environments

It is worth considering sometimes creating class dramas with classes in particular environments and landscapes, such as forests or beaches. Perhaps school journeys and trips can open up this imaginative possibility as part of the school journey experience. A drama about the Rainforest, for example, works well in a real forest (even if it has the wrong species) and a desert island drama of course is great to do on a beach or in sand dunes. Unit 5 in this book is a drama based around the Norfolk Broads, and a 'real' site visit would be very stimulating and informative. Of course, the increase in risk assessments for off-site activity and particular concern about children near water makes it necessary to plan any such drama activity well in advance and carry out formal risk assessments.

There is a current emphasis on increasing the use of the outdoor learning environment to help children learn across the whole curriculum and young children are spending more school time out of doors, often with teaching assistants specifically trained for working in this way. There is also a significant move through 'Forest Children' and 'Forest Schools' (brought across from

Scandinavia) to teach the whole curriculum out of doors within natural environments. Outdoor imagined worlds, dramatic play and drama can be an important part of this.

What shall I do about my role-play areas?

Most classrooms for Foundation and Key Stage 1 children have an area designated and designed to encourage and support role play. These areas seem to be becoming ever more interesting, imaginative and learning focused. Usually they link to a theme or area of learning that is being covered in the curriculum by the class, for example, a shop when the class focus is on money calculation, a travel agency maybe when the class is finding out about Europe, a Chinese restaurant when it is almost the Chinese New Year, a hospital when the class are finding out about Florence Nightingale, and so on. The possibilities are endless.

Involve the children in creating the role-play area, letting them suggest what could be put in it and asking them to bring in suitable props and costumes for the area. Invite them to suggest where different props and costumes might be placed in the area and see if they can justify their suggested positioning. This offers shared ownership of the area. It also means that you are taking account of the children's ideas and can be sure it includes what is of interest to them as well as your own ideas, for example, children might bring a bucket and spade or shells to leave in a seaside role-play area but the teacher might introduce the need to record and display the weather each day on the pretext of informing holidaymakers.

Adults may introduce role-play ideas but the associated tasks need to be passed over early to the children to do themselves. You will probably provide stimuli relevant to the area that will encourage speaking and listening, reading and writing, for example, a travel agent's computer, telephone, notepads, employee name badges, travel brochures, map of Europe, and so on. You might decide to have a role-play area that links to the whole-class drama and this would stimulate ongoing in-role activity after the drama lesson, for example, the role-play area could have real objects and an environment that represents or links to the sea and the inside of Billy's Bucket (Unit 2).

When a role-play area is new, children are very keen to get into it and have a turn. It is worth letting children just play freely in the area without an adult in role initially. Their attention will be drawn to the free-play possibilities to begin with, and you will find it more difficult to get their sustained attention when the area is new. There is no right or wrong period of time to leave role-play areas *in situ*. Observant adults will sense when the children are losing interest in the area and it is time to change it or raise the learning stakes with an 'in-role' dramatic challenge. The main thing is to make sure it is an area that is clearly valued and is full of stimulus and possibility.

The role of the adult in role-play areas

After a play session or two (when the play may well be becoming a little repetitive) you might consider arranging to get into the area alongside the children or briefing another empathetic adult to go in with a learning agenda. Before entering the play area, it is worth observing the children's play for a while and picking up what is already happening before slipping in as a co-participant in their dramatic play. If the children are not used to you going in alongside them, then you may ask them if it is alright for you to do so. They are unlikely to say no and it shows a respect for their play and signals that you will not be hijacking it.

As a role-play co-participant (and as a drama teacher) you look for opportunities to raise the level of dramatic tension, through presenting the children with problems to be solved (preferably collaboratively), in role.

In a role-play area you could:

- be a customer at the shop and say that you have forgotten your purse when you get to the till

- bring back an item past its sell by date and ask for a refund

- at the travel agency role-play area, ask which is the furthest away European country and say you are only prepared to go by train

- at the Chinese restaurant be the unhappy local fish and chip shop owner whose trade is suffering since their Chinese restaurant opened

- be the person who lives next door to the new restaurant and is being kept awake by customers coming and going until midnight.

What role you take and the challenge you set through it, will depend on what you want the children to experience, learn or practice. These in-role problem-solving opportunities with adults in role alongside children in role are a valuable way of introducing and developing real learning opportunities into children's dramatic play. The skills they are practising and developing stay with them after the role play is over.

Role play is the seedbed of drama in education, and the role of the empathetic adult underpins later 'teacher in role'. The drama teacher works alongside children in role but also introduces a range of established drama conventions and strategies to whole classes, in order to structure the learning and communication opportunities and provide drama forums.

What about drama clubs?

Drama clubs are desirable and are on the increase with the emphasis on extending the school day. However, they should be seen as an addition to drama lessons not a substitute for them. Clubs are not necessarily open to, or attended by, all pupils and so there is immediately an entitlement issue. Often attendance is hampered by other clubs at the same time or by children needing to catch after-school buses or meet other commitments. Sometimes drama clubs are age restricted. A school may have a drama club, but if in practice it is not open and accessible to all children then it can be a source of frustration to those who cannot attend.

There are different types of drama clubs and you need to be clear what the purpose of your drama club is and how it will differ from drama lessons. You will need to decide whether children have to commit for a length of time to attending or can attend on a casual basis. This may influence what the club offers and achieves. If you want to work towards a performance, you will need some level of guaranteed attendance. If you are providing drama workshops that are developmental, you may still want some consistency of attendees. If you are providing a series of one-off drama workshops or a club that is basically drama games, then children can perhaps just come to some sessions. Some drama clubs seem to make considerable use of drama games, with sessions consisting of little else. This is often because of constantly shifting attendance or children arriving and leaving at different times, which can make it difficult to sustain a drama. Sometimes it is because the person leading the club does not know what else to offer. The drama games might develop drama skills and no doubt children enjoy these clubs but it is questionable whether the children will develop much meaningful drama if the clubs just offer drama games. If drama clubs provide sustained drama and children have to contract into a certain regularity of attendance, what can be achieved of worth drama-wise is greater.

There are a growing number of theatre educators and drama workshop leaders making themselves available as external drama-club providers to schools. This links in with the workforce remodelling agenda. If the quality is good then this is worth considering. Ideally external providers should be prepared to work in close partnership with the school to offer more than a detached 'bolt on' drama experience. It may be that a group of schools together could consider setting up a drama club and share the cost of a good external provider to run drama in the extended school day at one school for attendees from several schools. Perhaps the same provider could provide several after-school drama clubs within a cluster of schools. Maybe a teacher with drama expertise could run a club that is open to other schools and reciprocal arrangements be made for other types of club elsewhere. Perhaps someone with drama expertise in the community can work with you (subject, of course, to enhanced CRB checks).

Why should we take children to the theatre?

> Children need to go to the theatre as much as they need to run about in the fresh air … the very limitations of theatre allow the audience to share in the acting … require the audience to pretend. It won't work if they don't. (Pullman, 2004)
>
> A theatre is the most important sort of house in the whole world because that's where people are shown what they could be if they wanted, and what they'd like to be if they dared to, and what they really are. (From Moominsummer Madness by Tove Jansson)

Children need to experience and respond to live theatre. Not only can theatre be a powerful cultural, personal learning experience but it provides models from which children can abstract techniques and ideas when devising their own drama and theatre. The more good theatre experiences children have, the greater the range of ideas and techniques they will build up in their memories, which they can draw on when they create their own dramas. They need to have the opportunity to experience theatre, respond to it personally and with others, and to evaluate it in order to make sense of it and understand what makes it powerful and effective. They then need to be able to use this knowledge to create effective drama and theatre themselves both within drama lessons and for other audiences.

Some schools have established good and sustainable relationships with local theatres, many of whom are funded increasingly to work with schools in the theatres and in the schools. It is valuable to have a sustained relationship with a theatre and perhaps be able to visit backstage, talk with directors and with actors about the play and their performances, and learn a little about the way plays are staged and theatres operate. Some touring theatre companies provide workshop opportunities to support the children's understanding of a play and give them the opportunity to work with professional actors and directors.

Sometimes small touring theatre groups are available to visit schools or groups of schools. Occasionally performances are subsidized by sponsors. Getting together with other local schools to buy in a theatre company will bring down the cost. It is worth spending some time checking in advance the quality of the theatre group's work. It is usually possible to ask them for the names of other schools they have visited recently and then to contact these schools to speak with the headteacher or drama subject leader before firmly booking. If your local authority has a drama or arts adviser, then you could ask for the names of theatre companies whose work is known to be of high quality.

As well as theatre groups available to work in schools, there are also theatre in education groups. These are companies that focus on the educational potential of theatre to support children's learning. The performances often are interactive, requiring various forms of participation from the class or school audience. Often there are class workshops available in school to follow up the performance with the children or teacher's packs that support the teacher to prepare and follow up the theatre performance.

Sometimes students at high schools and in further education colleges devise theatre performances for specific audiences as part of their examination courses. Sometimes these audiences are primary school children and this is a good local opportunity to see a piece of theatre. With children often recognizing the performers as neighbours and siblings, the message that theatre is something that is inclusive and accessible is given.

What about school plays?

Every child should have the opportunity to take part in school plays (preferably several school plays and some of their own devising). It is important in the primary school that productions are inclusive and give opportunity over time to all children as participants and not just those who shine at drama. It is not wise to force children on stage against their will, but devising plays with classes can enable all children to have a suitable part that is challenging without being too threatening. There are also opportunities for children to play instruments off stage or help operate lighting and sound, make tickets and posters, organize the 'front of house' and review the play. The main thing is to get everyone involved and feeling that they have an important part to play in the collective success of the performance.

Sometimes whole-school plays are thematic and involve each class working on scenes based on a theme that are then amalgamated as a collective performance. Sometimes performances can be about sharing work from drama lessons. If you decide to work from a published play script there is nothing to stop you from being creative with it and enabling the children to make it their own. A play script can be seen imaginatively as a springboard and not a straitjacket. Do remember that if you are performing the work of a playwright you probably will need to pay performance royalties.

Putting on a play is a great and memorable team experience, and a positive way to bring the local community into your school as audience or even co-actors. Alternatively, you can take your play out into the local community. Evaluating and reviewing performances in the making and afterwards is an important and valuable part of the whole process and experience.

CHAPTER 5

Planning 'Whole-Class' Drama

How do I decide what the drama will be about?

Drama can be about anything. With a statutory National Curriculum in place and a National Strategy Framework, you will probably have a clear idea of much that you want the children to learn about (because it has been prescribed), but the way in which they might learn it has become less prescriptive. So your lesson (or series of lessons) might well link to something that you have to teach anyway and is already part of your curriculum plan or map. Drama may be the way that you have decided to approach it this time. It may be the content, process or the skills that will underpin what you want the children to learn, experience and develop. It may be a combination of these aspects.

Supposing you decide that the children will learn about the Great Fire of London and will do so partly through drama (Unit 3). It is unlikely that *all* that you want them to learn will be best achieved experientially through drama. There may be aspects of the Great Fire that you will want to teach in ways other than drama in order to ensure coverage within curriculum time constraints. You will need to decide whether the drama will be an initial stimulus to get them interested in the Great Fire before they know anything about it, or whether the drama will start when the children already know a bit about the fire and can bring their knowledge to the drama. In practice it is often a bit of both, with children having some knowledge and understanding already that they bring to a drama lesson and then being motivated through the drama to find out more after the lesson, for example, a 7-year-old who decided that in her bakery in 1666 she was making doughnuts and then wondered whether doughnuts existed in 1666 and wanted to find out. Another child was washing her windows in the drama set in 1666 and wondered if there was glass then, and set about finding out. Decide the relative emphasis of different learning objectives within the drama lesson and often only some of these will be drama objectives, while others might be history or English objectives, for example diary writing. You might have personal, social, emotional, spiritual, cultural, creative objectives in mind as well as other subject objectives, but if it is a drama lesson then, logically, one would expect there always to be at least one main drama objective.

Where does the dramatic tension/interest lie?

When planning a drama you will need to consider where the moments of greatest dramatic tension lie. For example in a whole-class drama about the Great Fire the drama will not be just about acting out the story of the Great Fire, it will be about creating and actively engaging with key moments in role. Moments of dramatic tension might, for example, include any of the following:

- the moment the baker realizes that his house is on fire

- trying to persuade someone who is afraid of heights that they must step out onto the roof for safety

- deciding what possessions you value most and will carry with you

- striking a deal with a shifty boatman, to take you up the river to Greenwich

- trying to convince someone that their house will need to be pulled down as part of a firebreak

- deciding whether to slow down your escape from the fire by helping someone else

- being stuck at the bank of the Thames with the fire approaching and no boats available for hire.

Involve the children in the planning

This book contains units of work that are not set in tablets of stone. You can change the activities or select from them. You might ask the children to suggest possible key moments in advance of structuring and selecting for the drama, for example, ask them:

- What do you *know* about the Fire of London?

- What do you *think you know* about the Fire of London?

- What do you *wonder* about the Fire of London?

You could gather their responses and then you will have areas of interest that you can set up a structure for exploring. For example, children might wonder aloud and say, 'I wonder how many people died'. 'I wonder if there was looting.' 'I wonder if I had any relations from long ago that saw the fire.' 'I wonder if they let prisoners free or left them to burn.' 'I wonder what precious things got burned.' 'I wonder what happened to all the animals.' 'I wonder how everyone got food afterwards.'

You can see that with a little time to take on board what the children are already wondering there is plenty of material here from which to structure a drama lesson and, with a little time for research, it might be possible to find authentic information and text that could be woven into or start the lesson, for example:

I also did see a poor cat taken out of a hole in a chimney … with the hair all burnt off the body and yet alive … I went towards Islington and Highgate where 200,000 people of all classes lay down alongside the heaps of what they could save from the fire. His majesty and Council called a Proclamation for the rest of the country to come in and help to feed them. (Samuel Pepys' Diary, http://europeanhistory.about.com/od/ukandireland/a/apepysfire_4.htm)

The Resource Sheets 3 and 4 for Unit 3 are an example of this sort of authentic information that can fascinate the children and support the drama.

You will also want to stay alert to the children's spontaneous ideas that will become evident during the lesson and build on unpredicted moments of dramatic tension that arise when the lesson is under way. Having a plan is like having scaffolding for the lesson. It is just a flexible framework that can be rearranged if necessary. You can stick to your plan like glue, but the more you are able to take on board the children's emerging ideas, events and characters, the more they will feel a sense of engagement with, and ownership of, the drama. It is the children's ideas and responses that are the real meat of the lesson and are far more important than the pre-lesson plan.

You do not need to sacrifice your intended learning objectives in order to listen and respond to children's ideas and, if a gem of an idea comes unexpectedly, it would be foolish to ignore it for the sake of the plan as long as you end up returning at some point (maybe in a different lesson) to any objectives you have not met. If the teacher decides everything about the direction of the drama, then whose drama is it? Children are active learners not teachers' puppets.

This is not saying, 'Don't plan'. You do need to plan but as a springboard not as a straitjacket. Forward planning can mean that through the drama about the Great Fire you might also decide to cover within the drama lesson aspects of persuasive speech, diary writing, report writing, science work on fire, responding to art (paintings of the Great Fire), architecture and city planning, rivers, fire prevention, and so on. Forward planning also means that you enter the lesson with a big security blanket. The more inexperienced you are at teaching in and through drama, the more important it is to have a plan, which you may or may not stick to rigidly. The main thing is that the children are making progress in every drama lesson and not just being happily occupied. Also if you are teaching a subject through drama, the learning that the subject requires must not be sacrificed or diluted.

Also for any drama to sustain the interest of the children it will need to keep true to what the children themselves are interested in, so the aim is to ensure the children learn what they need to, in ways that engage them and take account of where their interest lies as the drama lesson progresses. This sounds quite a juggling act but it's perfectly possible to achieve as long as the adult is attentive to the way that the drama is developing and really listens to the children's ideas and weaves them through the drama with a constant eye on the intended learning.

What can help me structure a drama lesson?

You are not setting off into a drama void when you embark on teaching in and through drama. Inexperienced teachers often think of drama in terms of potentially wild and uncontrollable unstructured improvisation through which they will lose control of the children. They worry about behaviour and how to keep the class in the same drama. Drama, like theatre, needs at times to be highly disciplined, and whole-class drama can be highly structured with the amount of freedom offered being securely in the hands of the teacher. The skill is to let the drama reins out freely from time to time and then judge when to pull them back in and when to loosen them still further. If the children are engaged and keen for the drama to work they may be tugging at the reins for good purpose. Too often teachers' insecurities hold back the learning possibilities drama can provide.

Drama has a well-established bag of tools that you can use to structure the lesson and they are usually referred to as drama strategies or conventions. Some of them you will probably have heard of as they are in common parlance, particularly in schools, for example, hot-seating, freeze-frame, tableau. There is a section later in this book that lists several of the main drama strategies and briefly explains them (see pages 152–54). Strategies are tools and should be used to enable, to focus attention, to scaffold and to give form to an unfolding drama.

Drama strategies can be seen as individual ingredients in a drama cake. Alone the ingredients are not enough, and when put together they are more than the sum of their parts. A drama lesson is not just a variable string or sequence of strategies. Drama has to be about something and it has to be about something that engages the children and matters to them. It has to gain and keep their full attention, be relevant and have elements of dramatic tension.

How would I begin to plan a whole-class drama?

Good drama teaching has much in common with the basic principles of good teaching in any subject. It should grab and then sustain the interest of all children and move them on from what they already know and can do into new knowledge, skills and understandings. It should motivate them personally as learners to want to learn more and it should be enjoyable, challenging all pupils and enabling all pupils to achieve. Good drama involves setting up meaningful, albeit imaginary, contexts that support vivid, real learning. Drama lessons are not about children being superficially active and enjoying themselves but learning little that is new.

As well as learning about drama or learning about another curriculum area through drama, the children are also learning a great deal personally, socially and emotionally as well as culturally and creatively during drama. So when you are planning your drama lesson and you start by saying, 'What is it I want the children to experience and learn?', the objectives may be wide-ranging and not only drama-specific. The same source material or drama lesson can be changed to create different learning opportunities and outcomes depending on how you structure the lesson, where the emphasis lies and on how responsive you can be to what the children offer as the drama progresses.

Feel able to start with someone else's plan

Those new to teaching drama can be expected to start out with a lesson plan that may not be of their own devising. This book contains eight units of drama work that can be your starting point. Starting with a plan understandably makes the teacher or teaching assistant feel safer. Drama lesson plans can be considered to be a bit like recipes. When you start out cooking you cling to a recipe and when you start out teaching drama you might cling to a lesson plan. After you have experienced enough recipes (or drama lessons planned by others) to feel confident enough to tinker with the plan or even substitute the basic ingredients (or drama strategies and conventions) and see what happens as a result, then you might begin to get a little more adventurous. When being a bit adventurous works, you may decide to leave other people's lesson plans further and further behind you and more confidently devise more lessons of your own.

The real key to success is to:

- keep the drama where the children's interests lie

- get the pace right

- ensure that all children can participate

- take part yourself.

Sometimes you will be delighted by the outcome and sometimes you realize it is not really satisfying the children's appetite for learning and is not producing satisfactory drama. That is fine because we are on a voyage of professional discovery and we are evaluative practitioners. The important thing is not to give up but to work out what might need to now be done differently in the next lesson and then try again for a different outcome. It is an ongoing and exciting process of discovery as we learn increasingly what is most likely to engage the children in drama that will meaningfully develop their learning and extend their drama abilities. We have a powerful starting point. Most children love doing drama so motivation, particularly in the primary school is most often not an issue in drama lessons except where the teacher consistently offers the children either too much or too little freedom and challenge!

Drama, like any creative process, requires moments of free-flow but also needs structure and focus at times to achieve a worthwhile outcome. Look at how very structured and focused a theatre performance is! It is the teacher's job to make sure that structure and focus is provided within drama lessons too. Older and more experienced drama students can increasingly provide structure and focus themselves after experiencing and analysing what makes drama work well.

How do I introduce the idea of whole-class drama to children?

Drama is about pretending to be someone else, somewhere else, with something happening that is not really. If the children are not used to drama or they think it is only about putting on plays for an audience, then it is helpful to talk a bit about what they think drama is and what the shared expectations will be within the drama lesson. In order to explain whole-class drama you might ask them the following questions.

1. *Do you ever pretend to be someone else?* Most children readily agree that they do. Older children do but may not so readily admit it at first.

2. *Who do you do this with?* They usually say their friends or brothers and sisters and sometimes parents. Sometimes they say they do it alone.

3. *Do you ever pretend you are somewhere else?* Again, they usually say they do.

4. *Do you ever pretend that something is happening, when it is not really?* Yes, they will say again that they do.

Explain to the children that when they do this sort of 'pretend' or 'make-believe' activity, it is a type of drama. Drama is sometimes about putting on plays but it doesn't have to be. Drama is about pretending to be someone else, somewhere else, with something happening that is not really and it is usually done with other people. Tell them that the drama that you want them to try with you is more like the pretending that they do with their friends but that it might also involve some performing to each other in parts of the lesson. Also you might want to point out that drama is always a story and that sometimes drama stories are written down in a special way as play scripts but that the drama story that they will be doing will be made up as they go along by everybody pretending together. What happens will be up to them. Explain that you will be involved in this whole-class 'pretend' with them and will take an active part in the pretending.

What should the adult/s be doing during the 'whole-class drama'?

Just think about the way that an empathetic adult with a learning agenda for a young child interacts with them in dramatic play situations and you will be on the right path. During a whole-class drama you should be ready and willing to become a fellow participant, taking on a role in the drama from time to time and not just remain the detached organizer of the children's experiences. If you do not get involved in role then you will miss many golden opportunities to challenge and extend children's thinking from within the drama itself.

In early dramatic play the adult is a model who is imitated by the child, for example, mum or dad is cooking and the young child pretends to do the same alongside. The activity is companionable and it is also instructive. The adult may be empathetic and interactive, co-participating in the child's dramatic play and leading the play on, using it as a vehicle for chatting together and perhaps supporting the child's learning while having fun. The co-participation of the adult is not just pleasurable for the child as they have the adult's attention but is pleasurable also for the adult who is having an enjoyable and playful time bonding with the child. Through co-participation the adult is also giving a message (maybe not consciously) that they value make-believe activity. It is worthy of their time. They take it seriously.

How does 'playing alongside' translate into a drama setting?

Children are picking up all the time on messages about role play and drama. Whether or not there is a role-play corner or time allocated for drama lessons and whether empathetic adults clearly value dramatic play and drama and co-participate, give various and clear messages to children about the value placed on make-believe. Whether the role-play area is just somewhere they go when they have finished their mathematics and English or whether it is a place they go that involves mathematics and English also gives different messages. Whether one teacher values it and others do not also gives out messages. One teacher can work hard at raising the status of role play for another to undo that good work and marginalize it.

The teacher/teaching assistant needs to set up drama opportunities for the children but also ideally needs to involve themselves in role and be able to mediate the experience for the learner. Even if prescriptive lesson plans or radio programmes are being used to support the drama, it should be done *with* the children and not *to* them. If an adult is present, only directing and observing without co-participating, then this changes the dynamic of the lesson and the status of the relationship between the children and the adult. There may well be times when the teacher needs to give instructions and to direct, but the main thrust is to enable and facilitate, to help the children have and give form to their own ideas and not to just enact the teacher's ideas. The ownership of whole-class drama should lie with the whole-class and not just with the adult.

Drama, however, needs to be structured and the adult needs to support the structuring of the drama experience, particularly when children have little drama experience. Drama is not just an improvisational free for all. There are a wide range of flexible drama tools, strategies and conventions that can support the teacher in doing this structuring, but of course it is what is made with the tools that counts.

But *how* do I work in role with children?

The most powerful drama strategy there is for a teacher (or a teaching assistant) is to take on a role, interacting and working with children who are also in role. But despite this linking closely to playing dramatically alongside young children, the idea of taking on a role within a whole-class drama strikes fear unnecessarily into the heart of some adults or, conversely, brings out the frustrated thespian in others.

Always tell the children you will be working in role, even if they are used to you taking roles. If it is new to them then explain it, for example, 'In a moment I am going to pretend to be someone else and I'd like you to help me to pretend this'.

Give Teacher in Role (TiR) one or two short practices before trying to sustain a role (especially if TiR is new to you or the children), for example, by letting them briefly meet you pretending for a few minutes to be a character from a story.

Make it clear when you are in or out of role. You may wish to 'sign' you are in role by using a simple piece of costume or prop when you are, for example, 'When I carry this stick I am pretending to be the old man in the story'.

Make it clear that you are serious about being in role and try to mask any awkwardness you may feel. If the children sense that you are embarrassed, finding it difficult or not taking it seriously, then they will pick up on this and will also find it difficult to operate effectively alongside you in role.

Start off with a role you feel comfortable about playing. This is most likely to be a high-status role but do not avoid experimenting with different types and status roles, and be aware of the different ways that children respond to your different roles.

Decide what the purpose and function of your role is in relation to the children's learning and be sensitive to when it is no longer necessary for you to be in role. You can go back into role again whenever you need to.

You do not have to keep to one role throughout a whole drama. Sometimes taking on different roles at different points in the drama for different purposes can be more productive.

Do not get carried away acting and forget the children! If the teacher exhibits a powerful personal performance it can disempower the children, make them lose confidence to contribute and marginalize them. You do not need to be a great actor to do teacher in role but you do need to do it with seriousness and commitment.

So how do I choose a role for myself?

Think about what you want the role to achieve for the children and for the drama. If you think about roles as mainly having two functions, *information-giving roles* and *information-gathering roles*, then this will help you to select a role.

For example if there is a fictional place that is being established in a drama the teacher might decide to be:

- A *visitor to the kingdom*, asking the children about life in this kingdom. This is a way of *gathering* and sharing the children's ideas and building up belief in the kingdom and gives ownership of it to the children. Being more knowledgeable than the visitor the children may feel confident to speak up about the kingdom. A visitor is typically a low-status role.

- *The king*. This could be a way of *giving* the children information about the kingdom, its laws and customs. As royal subjects in the presence of the king they may feel intimidated about speaking. A king is typically a high-status role.

- *The king's messenger*. This could be a flexible, intermediary role, used for *giving and gathering* information. The messenger can give information to the people from the king and gather information as a fellow subject or on behalf of the king. A messenger is typically a mid-status, intermediary role.

It is also useful to think about the status of the teacher in the role selected, particularly in relation to the children's roles. The three roles also each have different status and will each set up a different dynamic. A child as a villager in a kingdom will hopefully feel and respond differently towards the king, his messenger or a visitor. Of course, it will depend how the roles are played. It is possible to use teacher in role to break down and challenge stereotypes. The drama will evolve differently if the king is played in different ways. A kindly and benevolent king will elicit a different response from a tyrannical one. A messenger who is trusted will gather different information from a messenger who is not. A visitor who is secretive will get a different response from a visitor who is open and communicative. So you need to decide the purpose and function of the role, the status of the role and how you will play it. You also need to decide how you will 'sign' the role, how children will know when you are in or out of role and who you are pretending to be. The children need to be very clear about their role in the drama too, in order to respond appropriately.

Before being able to work in role, both teachers and children need to know:

- Who am I? (character)

- Who are they? (character)

- Where are we? (setting)

- What is the situation at this moment? (plot/dramatic tension)

But most of all you just need to give it a try, even if just for a few minutes at a time. You can come out of role and talk with the children about how it went and hopefully thank them for helping you to stay in role.

How do I decide roles for the children ... or do they decide?

Children should have experience of working in role:

- individually

- in pairs

- in groups

- as a whole class

- with the teacher in role.

It is best to avoid many different roles being given out to individuals among a class of children, particularly younger children. It is often more effective to set up generic 'collective'-type roles through which the children then create, adopt and develop particular characteristics and characters. Particularly when setting out on whole-class drama with young children, it works best if they are all similar roles, for example, *all* going into the underwater world or storyland together, *all* villagers trying to outwit a Samurai warrior, *all* Londoners fleeing the Fire. Also it works with very young children if they are a singular Collective Role, that is, all are one character, for example, all can be Billy's friend who is guarding his bucket (Unit 2). If roles are over-differentiated too early it becomes a bit complicated, too challenging for the children and the teacher, and difficult to manage. When you start out with drama and when children are starting out with drama keep it simple and keep it clear. Gradually you can weave in more characters and complications.

How does my role influence theirs?

What role you decide to take as teacher in relation to the children's roles changes the dynamics and opens up different possibilities and learning opportunities. You will want to consider what you want the children to learn and achieve through the role they have been given and what your role can do to help this. Maybe you want them to be talking to a bullied mermaid because you want to find out what advice they will offer her (Unit 2). Maybe it is because you want them to sequence her journey back across the seabed to her home. Maybe you just want them to engage with key moments of dramatic tension in the plot or become curious about what else the Bully Fish may have done that has not been told. Maybe you will want them to question the mermaid to improve their questioning skills or to stimulate a piece of report writing later. You may wish them to engage with any or all of these purposes or just decide to sense where the children's interest in the story lies and use that as a vehicle for the drama and for learning.

It is helpful to think about roles as flexible rather than fixed. We need to free ourselves from the notion of always having to sustain the same role throughout the drama and realize that in drama we can creatively go in and out of the same or different roles by agreement. We can share one role at the same time or at different times by passing on the role to someone else. Also one role can be played simultaneously by a group of children and different roles can be played by different groups of children, for example, a group is the wolf and another group is Grandma. This is sometimes called Collective Role or Collective Voice. It spreads the joy or burden of a key role among a group of children and encourages them to listen carefully to each other and to co-operate and support each other in order to make the role convincing. They need to pay attention to each other to make sure that they really sound as if they are one and the same character. Another advantage of sharing key roles in this way is that it not only encourages engagement with key characters, but it also guards against unrealistic demands being placed on one child to sustain a key role and the jealousy and demotivation this can lead to among other children, that is, 'I am annoyed and not interested now because he's got the part I wanted'.

It is possible to structure dramas so that children can select and develop their own roles within an overall context. They can, for example, all be Londoners in 1666 but can also develop separate sub-roles, for example, one child might be a baker, another a rich merchant, another a pickpocket. They are supported and bound together as Londoners facing a fire but are able to develop an individual, pair or group role within the confines of that.

Starting the drama: what shall I use as the opening 'hook'?

The start of any lesson is very important. It's a special moment that needs the full attention of the class and a drama lesson benefits from a clear start for dramatic effect. Even if you have had to shift desks, deal with latecomers and do the register first, you need to make a clear lesson starting point and not just drift seamlessly into it. That is why moving into another space helps, but even if you are in the classroom doing drama, you can still make the starting moment important and anticipatory.

You will become alert to all sorts of stimuli for starting drama

- a newspaper article
- a piece of evocative music
- a picture book
- a painting
- linked sounds
- poems
- photographs
- log books
- historical documents
- a real object supposedly belonging to a fictional character
- ideas from the children themselves

Start drama lessons in a range of ways over time

- sometimes visually (maybe with a painting, photograph or sculpture)

- sometimes aurally (maybe through a poem read aloud or a piece of music)

- sometimes tactilely (through passing around a significant object or artefact)

- sometimes kinaesthetically (through mime or movement)

What is likely to engage the interest of all children in the class from the outset and keep them curious?

For example:

- an ambiguous image

- a letter from an imaginary character

- the teacher taking on a role at the start

- atmospheric music

- a drama focused immediately on something that already interests them.

Think about how much they need to know in order to get started

Avoid talking for too long *about* the drama before they actually start working in role and actively making the drama!

Remember you do not have to start at the beginning!

The first drama lesson around a theme or topic can start at any point in the drama and we can then go back in time and find out what has happened before through flashback. Drama does not have to be linear in form. It can build up like a jigsaw puzzle that can start anywhere. You can dip in and out at places and build up the big picture gradually.

Try to make sure that the children start securely and can achieve what you are asking fairly easily at the start

Children doing drama need to feel successful and challenged. A strategy that invites participation and does not make too many public demands on any individual child is a good opener. Unit 3 in this book is about the Great Fire of London but you could decide to start a drama on this theme differently. There are many ways that you could start and here are just a few:

- *You could start by* asking the children (maybe in advance of the lesson itself) to suggest what scenes a drama about the Great Fire might have in it (but not commit to using them ... the word is *might*). Allow them only a sentence that gives possible scenes a title. This will help you gauge where their interest lies and give time for some planning.

They might say that it could have scenes about, 'Putting the fire out', 'Seeing your house burn', 'Rescuing people', and so on. You will need to find a way of engaging them with the whole-class drama, making it challenging and meaningful as the drama develops. Do not let them give you a narrative, for example, 'I think we should do a drama about a baby getting left in a house on fire and this other lady goes into the house and rescues it and decides to keep it. Then later on the real mother sees the baby and says, "That's my baby" … ' and so on. You do not want the drama being scripted by yourself or a dominant child and then the other children just enacting someone else's narrative. You want to get it started with a world of possibility ahead and the children knowing that anything is possible in this drama as it evolves. The drama belongs to every child.

■ *You could start by* looking with them at a famous painting or etching of the Great Fire as a stimulus (see Resource sheet 2). Other pictures of the Great Fire are easy to find on the Internet through an image search. You could show a painting of the Great Fire to the children (possibly using an interactive whiteboard) and ask them to play the 'I wonder game', for example, 'I wonder who the man at the front of the picture is, who is covering up his belongings … I wonder if those people can feel the heat from where they are'. We do not need answers yet; we just need to engage them and bring out the children's natural curiosity. The children are strictly speaking not in drama mode yet as they are not working in role, but they are engaging with the setting within which the drama will take place and posing questions that the drama may answer.

■ *You could start by* using 'teacher in role' as it is a highly engaging start to any lesson. You could start by telling the children that you are going to pretend to be Samuel Pepys and that you will be reading them an extract from your diary (see Resource sheet 4) after which they can ask you questions and you will answer in role. They might ask for example: 'What sorts of things had people taken with them. What did you see in their heaps of possessions?' 'What happened to your house?' Of course, when you are trying to stay true to historical fact and evidence you may well be asked questions that you do not readily know the answer to when you are in role. This is not a problem. You can answer in role, making it up and when you come out of role you can say to the children that they will need to check the accuracy of whatever you were not sure of, for example, 'When I was pretending to be Pepys and you asked if my own house was damaged in the fire I said it wasn't but I am not sure if that is true so we may need to find that out before the next lesson'. In fact asking the children to decide what you said in role that was 'true' and what was imagined by you, is a valid enquiry activity anyway outside the drama lesson.

■ *You could start by*, after the fire has happened, telling the children that you are an artist who has been commissioned to make a detailed painting (or series of paintings) of the Great Fire and it is important that you are as accurate as you can be. They were there on the banks of The Thames and saw at first hand what happened. They have information that you require to give detail to your painting. What scenes do they think should be depicted in your painting? Can they show you in groups what it was like? Can they bring the scene to life so that you can imagine that you are actually there? You can build up the painting as a tableau with all the scenes in it and bring one at a time to life, maybe silently, maybe with the speech of the characters or maybe with their thoughts and fears.

■ *You could start by* pretending that you are an artist or a writer, an investigator, an architect, an official trying to improve firefighting or any other professional with a reason to ask about the fire from the children in role.

■ *You could start by* presenting them with a real picture (tableau) of the Great Fire of London as the starting point and ask them to imagine that they are travelling into the picture as a character within it. You could ask them to place themselves somewhere in the room as if the room is the picture and they are motionless within it. In turn people enter a defined space and add themselves to the picture in silence as someone in the scene. This could be accompanied by an atmospheric musical background. They can then silently be asked to decide a little about themselves as you guide them in developing the role by saying something like: 'Know what your name is and what your trade is. Know where have you just come from. I wonder what the worst thing you have seen so far today is? I wonder what your biggest worry is at this moment. In a moment I will pass by each of you and when I am nearest to you say your name and give me any thought that your character is having at this moment.'

Shall I start with a warm-up/drama game?

Some drama teachers seem to spend a relatively long time doing drama warm-up activities and games before getting down to the drama itself without always analysing whether it is worth the time it takes away from the main focus of the lesson. If there is a particular reason why the children may need to do a 'warm-up' activity before getting going on the lesson 'proper' then fine, but this is not often the case.

A possible reason for a warm-up activity might be to get the whole class working cohesively together and paying attention to each other before entering roles, for example, moving around as a whole class and trying to all stop still at the same moment. This can only be achieved by a significant level of whole-class co-operation and 'sensing' the group. Tell them that a group that can co-operate well enough to achieve simultaneous stillness will have shown that they have the skills they need to co-operate well in drama too. When children achieve this collective stillness, they then feel confident that they can work well together, which will benefit the drama.

A warm-up activity may be a way of getting the children into drama mode and distancing themselves from whatever they have been doing previously. If they have rushed in from a windy playtime then they may need a stilling activity, a cool-down rather than a warm-up. Conversely, if they have been sat still through the previous lesson, they may need an activity to get them moving before sitting again. If you do decide to do a drama warm-up then try to make it link in some way to the forthcoming drama itself, for example, 'Move if …' (Unit 7, Activity 1).

At the start of a lesson it is likely that the children are at their most attentive once they have settled, and to spend too much of the drama lesson just preparing to move on to the drama itself can be time-consuming and unproductive. Lesson time can run out for the drama itself because too much time has been spent on warming up instead of getting going.

If the drama games occur too often and are too 'fun'-based then it can be difficult to shift the children mood wise into serious and deep engagement with a role in a sustained fiction. They may just want to keep playing games, and teachers who are hesitant about actually getting on with a whole-class drama (which is more demanding) may go along with them and delay or avoid the drama itself. It is important to realize that drama games are not often themselves meaningful drama and they can overexcite the children and give the message that drama is games.

How do I make sure they do not just mess about when I start to do drama?

Ask the children what messes up pretending. They will know as they will have had experience of pretend situations falling apart, usually because not everyone tries to keep it going or because someone deliberately sabotages it! Sometimes the pretend is just not interesting enough to keep everyone on board. You will probably need to come to an agreement with the children about them trying together to keep the drama going. You can say that drama is a bit like a balloon that we try to keep up in the air between us through teamwork. Anyone can deliberately pop the drama balloon and mess up the game for everyone. That is easy but selfish and unfair to others. Tell them that the skilled thing to do is to work together to keep the drama balloon up in the air … and you know they can do it.

Nothing succeeds like success and when children engage emotionally with a drama that is being sustained and is rewarding they experience the power and excitement of drama and are affected by it. This becomes an intrinsic motivator that spurs them on to make the drama lessons work. They know the lessons will not work if people muck about and do not do the drama seriously. Children will begin to apply peer pressure to each other if they feel that a drama that is working and that they co-own is under threat from their classmates' silly behaviour.

What basic drama 'ground rules' or 'drama contract' do we need to have agreed before we start?

Do the children know the behavioural expectations of them during drama lessons? Having explained to the children the type of dramatic activity that you will be engaging in together you may wish to agree certain ground rules together that will constitute what you could call the 'Drama Contract'. Really a drama contract is a type of social behaviour contract and needs to be co-owned and agreed by everyone rather than imposed. You might ask what they think needs to be agreed by everyone before the drama starts or you could draw up or acquire a draft drama contract (Baldwin, 2004) as the basis of negotiation. You may decide to together add a sentence or two to an existing class behaviour contract that you already have agreed with the children.

It is very likely that you will already have a contract in place for Circle Time that is very close to what is required. Jenny Moseley, who has pioneered Circle Time in schools, is a trained drama teacher and circle time is based on the work of Jacob Moreno, who founded socio-drama and psychodrama. So if you have a Circle Time contract you almost have a drama contract, as they are almost the same. Turn-taking, respect for the contributions of others, and active and supportive listening are skills of co-operative Circle Time and whole-class group work (which whole-class drama of course is). What is different about drama is that it operates through taking on roles and pretending, and pretending can be a fragile thing. Therefore you need to add to any group working contract you already have that the children (and you) need to make sure that no one ever deliberately breaks the 'pretend' or 'make-believe' for someone else. They should all agree to try to keep the drama balloon up in the air! If they start to slip with the contract, just say, 'Balloon' and they will know what you are referring to.

The drama contract

A drama contract like any other behaviour contract should be positively framed rather than full of 'Don'ts' and might end up looking something like this:

When we are doing drama we agree that we will:

- Take the drama seriously, try hard to stay in role and pretend that the drama is real

- Help each other to keep the drama going and not do anything deliberately that could break the make-believe and spoil it for everyone else who is trying

- Encourage each other and not make fun of anyone in role or deliberately embarrass anyone during the drama (or after it)

- Listen to and watch each other carefully and respectfully

- Try to respond appropriately to each other in role

- Give each other and everyone opportunities to share ideas without putting anyone or their ideas down

- Give each other and everyone opportunities to speak and be involved

- Not hold anyone responsible out of the drama for what their character says or does in the drama – at the end of the drama session we go back to just being ourselves

- Agree that whatever anyone says or does in role belongs to the character and not the person pretending to be that character

---

Having a drama contract in place makes shared expectations clear and gives a sense of security to participants. You may need to remind children of the drama contract from time to time and, as with any contract, review it occasionally. Some teachers display the contract so that it can be referred back to directly if required.

What basic control signals will I need during the lesson?

Drama lessons are the same as any other lesson in some ways. You will need to make sure that the children respond readily to two basic signals.

First, you will need a signal that lets the children know that you want them to stop what they are doing instantly and be completely still and silent

- In order to be sure that both you and the children know that you still have full class control during the drama lesson as in any other lesson.

- To ensure the health and safety of the participants.

- So that you can halt the dramatic action at any point in the drama in order to hold a moment still (as in a freeze-frame).

You could just shout 'Freeze' or use an instrument that the children know means stop and be still, for example, a particular drum beat or a cymbal crash.

Second, you will need a signal that means 'Please find a suitable moment to stop what you are doing and give me your full attention'

- To leave the exact moment for halting the action in the hands of the participants themselves.

- To prevent frustrating the children by cutting their speech and/or actions short at an unsuitable moment.

The signal is up to you but maybe you stand with your arm in the air and the children will do the same when they are ready. This spreads quickly around a classroom and you do not need to use your voice. Or again you may designate an instrumental sound that means this, for example, a cymbal roll or shaking a tambourine.

How is it best to have the children positioned at the start?

Often teachers start with the children in a circle (as there is no hierarchy of space, even for the teacher and all people can see each other). Sometimes the children just gather round the teacher (which retains a spatial hierarchy). It is up to you, but sitting at desks as for other lessons is not ideal if you can avoid it.

The physical space the children inhabit in relation to you and to each other can easily influence the amount of attention they give the drama and their willingness to contribute.

- Who is sitting near whom and what is the likely impact of this?

- Is the way the children are seated helpful, neutral or a hindrance to starting the drama?

- Are there social groupings you might wish to alter by stealth through the use of a drama game that changes who the children are sitting near? for example, Fruit Bowl.

Fruit Bowl – a Drama Game

Each child in a circle is told consecutively that they are either apple, orange, banana or pear. When you call out the name of a fruit, all children who are that fruit must change places. When you call Fruit Bowl or Fruit Salad all children change places.

Teaching point

If you finish on Fruit Bowl or Fruit Salad you will find the children move back to be near their friendship groups, so do not finish on this if you want them to end up near different children and probably gender mixed.

It is preferable to use an activity to change groupings rather than to tell children to move away from people you do not want them working near or they may start the lesson feeling irritated and you will find convincingly shifting role from teacher to character more difficult.

Well-structured, compelling drama lessons with teachers who are confident, do not generally result in misbehaviour or lack of attentiveness, because engaged children are motivated and working deep in their interest zone and yet at the edge of their comfort zone keeps them alert. Once they have tasted drama working well, they will want the drama to work and will coerce each other into working seriously for that outcome.

Keeping the drama going: how do I decide the next drama move?

When you start teaching drama you will have probably produced a fairly detailed lesson plan in advance. As you become more experienced you will learn to be flexible and adapt planning in response to what the children and the unfolding drama requires. However, there are some basic guidelines to keep in mind that will probably influence your choice of strategies and conventions:

■ *When teacher in role is used, be sure that you are clear about the purpose of the role and what you want it to achieve*, so that you will know when it is time to come out of role.

■ *Will you be a 'teacher in role' (TiR) and, if so, what will you do or say to prepare the children and ensure they know when you are in or out of role?* Will you just tell them first or will you use a piece of costume, sit on a particular chair or carry a prop to signal when you are in or out of role? Children not used to a teacher working in role are likely to need some explanation and practice first (maybe just a couple of minutes at a time). It is disturbing if your teacher suddenly behaves as someone else with no explanation, especially to young children and those with particular difficulties, for example, those on the autistic spectrum, so *always make it clear you are in role and be sensitive to the children's response to this.*

■ *Think about different types of learner accessing the drama and use a range of activities that are visual, auditory, kinaesthetic, tactile.* This increases the likelihood of all pupils engaging, makes the experience more vivid and therefore more memorable.

■ *Make sure that children have opportunity to move as well as be static.* If the last move involved the children being still and seated, then you might wish to enable them to get up and move next (or vice versa). Try to avoid too much drama that keeps them in their chairs or on the mat for long periods of time. It is not just drama in the head, it should be in the body too!

How is it best to group the children?

Decide what group size best suits what you are trying to achieve for the drama and for the children themselves and give opportunity over time for working individually and in groups of different sizes and with different members.

Whole-class drama involves the class working as a whole class interactively together in the same scene at the same moment, for some and often much of the time, but it can also involve working individually in role and in groups of various sizes within the same overall whole-class fiction.

If the last move was whole class then decide if the next move also needs to be or whether what you want to achieve next can be done less or more effectively if the children now work in groups, pairs or individually. It is not necessary to ensure that all lessons have opportunities for individual, paired, group and whole-class work but it is worth just being aware that we sometimes slip into setting things up in the same way and the same children get together and the group dynamics become comfortable and predictable rather than challenging them to relate and work with different children.

Also what is demanded of children cognitively, socially and linguistically when working individually is different to what is demanded of them as a member of a small group or as part of a whole class. In drama we can shift easily between groups of various sizes during a lesson and keep up the level of challenge.

If they have been working in groups, maybe you now need to come up with a way of enabling all the groups to share their work with each other, for example, Performance Carousel.

Performance Carousel

Each group of about four children has a very short group scene or a still image, ready to present. The groups are then given a performance order. The teacher explains that everyone will start off as 'still as a photograph' on the ground. At an agreed signal (maybe a tambourine shaking or a visual signal), Group 1 first, slowly moves into a still, starting position and then after a few still moments the scene comes to life for just a few seconds and then freezes again, is held still again and melts. After Group 1 has been melted and still for 5 seconds, Group 2 starts to move slowly, taking their turn in the performance cycle, and so on.

With (5) meaning 5 seconds, you could describe the process to them as:

'Still (5) – Slow grow (5) – Freeze (5) – Action – Freeze (5) – Melt'

Teaching points

Challenge the children to all stop and start at *exactly* the same time.

Children waiting their turns will be on the floor and yet must remain *totally still and totally quiet*.

Ask them to imagine that they are all on stage even if it is not their group's turn to perform. Any movement that draws our attention away from the performers is a distraction to the audience.

Tell them that it is as if they are in the dark on stage and waiting for the spotlight.

One of the advantages of teaching the children how to do a Performance Carousel is that you will not need to set it up every time and will soon just be able to say, 'We will show this using Performance Carousel'. If you are firm and consistent about the teaching points, you will soon find you have an economic and theatrical way to bring together group performances with clear expectations.

Should I change the groups during the lesson or keep them the same?

If the children have been working in groups, will it be beneficial or not at this stage to ask them to all change groups so that they are working with others (thus changing the dynamics) or is there a good reason, to do with the drama or with the children, for leaving the groups unchanged?

An opportunity to interact in groups of different sizes changes the dynamics of the experience and changes the demands and the levels of challenge for individual participants. Small group work is usually best in groups no larger than four and it is best to change the constituency of the groups from time to time in order to not let the group dynamics become too fixed with the same children taking the lead position. Being expected to work with different children sometimes brings different challenges and opportunities and is good 'life skills' practice.

If the children have been working individually or in pairs then maybe you need a strategy that lets each person share a little of what they have just created. You could do this through Eavesdropping.

Eavesdropping

This simply involves listening in to 'in-role' conversations in a stylized way. It enables the whole class to listen in. Maybe a whole circle of children have been talking in role to partners or maybe groups have improvised scenes. Eavesdropping helps us find out what everyone else has been saying. The teacher can move around the outside of the circle of now silent children (or between the groups). When the teacher is nearest to any group or pair of

(Continued)

(Continued)

children, it is a signal that they alone may speak and be heard (until he or she moves on to stand near to the next pair or group of children). The teacher and whole class just hear snippets of each other's conversations and scenes.

Teaching points

Insist on total stillness and quiet from waiting groups. This helps ensure that they can see and listen to each other.

Do not spend too long in one place. This is just collecting snippets of what is being said.

You can ask the audience to close their eyes and touch participants on the shoulder when it is their turn. This supports focusing on sounds and words only, and can aid concentration.

Maybe a visual signal can help signal when the children should be speaking, for example, the teacher pretending to turn a huge volume knob up and down near each group or pair in turn, or an object such as a pretend travelling microphone carried by the teacher.

If the children have been working and interacting as a whole class together, then you may wish to hold the drama still for a moment for reflection, maybe by using a Freeze-frame and then listen to their in role thoughts, that is, through Thought-tracking.

Freeze-frame

Freeze-frame is almost self explanatory. You halt the action with a signal that everyone knows, maybe just through calling out 'Freeze!', and a moment in the drama is held still. It almost as if someone pressed the pause button. This is different to setting out to devise or create a still image deliberately. Freeze-frame gives you a still image but it was not discussed and planned as such in advance. It just happens to be how it looked at the moment the drama pause button was pressed. You might bring the action to life again, as if your finger has come off the pause button. Use any signal you have agreed with the children, for example, 'Action' or an instrumental signal.

Teaching points

Freeze needs to mean 'perfectly still'. Don't accept children fidgeting. They need to hold themselves in a position that is 'as still as a photograph'.

You might progress to the children deciding the moment they will all freeze the action. The challenge is for them to all agree when the moment is and manage to all freeze simultaneously without someone calling 'Freeze'.

Thought-tracking

This involves hearing a character's inner thoughts at a particular moment in the drama. This is usually done when a moment is held still (maybe through a freeze-frame). The teacher might say that when he or she is standing nearest to a particular person that they can speak their character's inner thoughts aloud for everyone to hear. You might also signal someone's turn to speak by touching them lightly on the shoulder, although teachers are more hesitant nowadays to make any physical contact with children. Sometimes there is a mismatch between what a character is thinking and has said previously. This is interesting to highlight, 'Why might a character say one thing but think something else?'

Teaching points

It is important to make sure that those speaking the thoughts can be heard by everyone. They may speak just to you and not be heard by others.

Thought-tracking is like a short soliloquy.

Drama teaching should enable children to truly work co-operatively and interactively as members of groups and as a whole class. Often what masquerades as group work in schools is no more than children sitting together in groups, doing the same thing as their group but in an isolated way. Drama demands truly interactive group work and cannot really work otherwise. If children are asked to create a group still image or improvisation that involves all group members, then it can only be achieved through the active participation, interaction and co-operation of the whole group. A good example of truly interactive group work can be found in a strategy called 'Collective Voice'. This is sometimes called 'Collective Role.' Collective Voice or Collective Role is a good way of sharing ownership of characters and getting all children to actively engage with a character and contribute to the character's development.

Collective Role/Collective Voice

This involves groups or even the whole class all speaking in role as the same character. They take turns to speak but try to give the impression that the same character is speaking. They might stand near each other or physically connect with each other to signal that they are one character. It means that a main part can have shared ownership rather than be given to one person to play.

Teaching point

Point out that the children must listen carefully to each other, otherwise inconsistencies will arise in what the character is saying. Accent or dialect is not important. It is consistency relating to the character that is important.

How can I make sure my lesson is balanced?

When drama is being planned, it is worth paying attention to a mixed provision of individual, paired, small group and whole-class work over time. Do not get straitjacketed by this as a lesson structure, as not all lessons need to have all permutations, just be aware that varying group size and composition inevitably make different demands and offer different opportunities. It is worth ensuring that groups (particularly if children select them for themselves) do not remain fixed for too long and that children do not end up always working with the same group. When this is the case the group dynamics become rather fixed and the same children may lead or follow the more domineering class members. If you can use reasons from within the drama itself for changing group composition and size then this is preferable to organizing the groups externally as the teacher, for example, 'Now one villager from each group is going to move to the next villager's group and tell them what rumours they have heard' is preferable to, 'Could one person from each group go to a new group so that you get the chance to work with someone else.' The first approach is likely to arouse interest and keep the dramatic tension going, whereas the second approach is more likely to lead to grumbles and complaints about having to move groups.

What should the teacher be doing during the lesson?

Listen and observe constantly

What are the children saying and doing that you as the teacher can pick up on and use in the evolving drama?

Be accepting of any or all ideas offered that are sincerely given by the children

Ignore any ideas that are offered flippantly. You do not have to use all the ideas offered, but you do need to be accepting of them in the signals you give. If children know their ideas are listened to and valued, they will think it worth trying to have still more ideas. If they think their ideas are not taken account of, they will stop bothering to offer them.

Ensure that the children are offered some (increasing) ownership of the drama

If the children think they are just expected to try and guess what the teacher's own idea is then they might set themselves up to fail and will not feel ownership of the drama. It is their ideas being used and shaping the drama that gives them the ownership. In time they may even begin to offer the structure, drama strategies and conventions, as they begin to understand how drama works.

Select in your mind which ideas the children offer (in and out of role) that can be used to support or shape the next part of the drama

Avoid abandoning the learning objectives.

Be aware of and responsive to their level of engagement and the lesson pace

Be sensitive to an activity going on too long and the children becoming disengaged and bored. Also, be sure that the drama demands you are making are challenging but not too difficult. It is often children who feel they are failing and children who are bored who misbehave. Are the children still fully engaged and are they being supported to take some ownership of the drama? The more ownership they can have, the more creative they can be. The more relevant to them the drama is, the more motivated and engaged they will be and the more they will learn and remember.

Make sure all children are getting opportunities to contribute

Are there children who are not contributing? Is every child engaged? If not, how can you help include all children and deepen their engagement? For example, ask a direct question to them in role that requires an 'in-role' response. Work alongside them or deploy another adult or child to work alongside them interactively in role.

Are one or two children dominating? This is often the case, so use a strategy to keep this in check, for example, use a 'Speaking Object'. Only the person holding the agreed object is empowered to speak at a particular time. It is better to try to stay 'in drama mode' and use drama conventions to deal with children's under- or over-enthusiastic behaviours and to ensure equal opportunity, than to, say, slip in and out of role as teacher and say, 'No, you have had a turn and it's someone else's turn now'. You may need to at times, but if the drama can do it for you that is preferable because it keeps the drama going rather than breaking the fiction to deal with unwanted behaviours. For example, if a class is being noisy, rather than ask them to quieten down you might, in role, tell them that they need to work quietly for a reason to do with the drama itself, for example, 'Try not to disturb other people on this ship. There are sick children on board and they need their sleep' or 'Don't let the Captain hear what you are saying to each other'.

Speaking Object

This is used to enable every child to have the opportunity to speak. Any object can be used, for example, a shell or a pen. It is sometimes worth having an object that links to the drama theme. Whoever holds the object is empowered to speak. The holder of the object speaks and then democratically passes the object on so someone else can speak next.

Teaching point

This involves accepting a ritual and associated rules. You can used 'Speaking Object' when you want to add ritual to the drama for significance, for example, every child can talk into a shell in turn to give support to the mermaid who has been bullied (Unit 2). However, you may just wish to use this device to stop a few children dominating and to make sure that every child has an opportunity to speak at a key moment.

Look for an opportunity and reason to raise the status and self-esteem of a particular child or children through the drama

For example, ask a child who seldom is chosen by peers, to carry out an important task in role within the drama and then praise them publicly for it.

Make sure the children have an opportunity to do more in drama than speaking and listening

Are they all getting an opportunity to contribute to the drama verbally and through movement and gesture? Drama might be in English but it is much more than just speaking and listening. Drama should not feel like a literacy lesson that just happens to use role. It should employ the body and mind and be an aesthetic and artistic experience.

Think as the drama unfolds ... where does their interest and the dramatic tension lie at this point in the drama?

If you are accepting and using the children's ideas, then you are not just following a drama recipe (although do so if you need to when you are new to drama but then get gradually a little braver). Be alert to what is making the children most curious and excited. Ask yourself, *'What is now of most importance at this particular moment to the children and to the drama and how can I help them explore it more deeply?'* You might actually ask the children to reflect on and speak about what they think is most important at different points in the lesson.

Questions you might ask when deciding which strategy might be most appropriate to deepen or move the drama on

- What is it we most want to (or need to) find out about in this drama now?

- Who in the drama might be able to help us find out? (Character.)

- Which character do the children think we most need to meet (or become, or watch) in the drama now and why? (The teacher and/or children can then become that character.)

- Where in the drama might we need to go to find out more? (Setting/plot.)

Drama teachers sometimes ask the children to place their thinking at a particular point in the drama into three columns.

What do we know? (Reference)	What do we *think* we know? (Inference and deduction)	What do we *want* to know? (Exploration)
How do we know it?	What makes us think we know this?	What are we curious about?
What evidence is there?	What stops us being sure?	Why might this be arousing our curiosity?
The first column reveals what the children are certain about	*The second column* shows what they are inferring or deducing from the drama so far	*The third column* reveals to the teacher what the children are wondering about and where their interest and the tension lies at this point. This acts as a guide for the teacher as to where the drama might focus next

At this point in the drama ...

It is possible for the children to share their ideas individually or in groups on paper (possibly using self-adhesive labels that allow statements to be moved between columns) but equally their ideas can be made physical. The drama space can be divided into three floor areas that represent the columns. Each child has an opportunity to place themselves physically in a column, speaking aloud the sentence instead of writing it.

The teacher then needs to decide what drama strategies to offer next, either to assist reflection, to go deeper with the same moment or to move the drama forward.

What happens if the drama lesson is going badly?

Do not worry! Remember that any drama lesson can be halted at any point and if necessary re-started, rewound and replayed. Do not feel that you need to carry on to the bitter end with a drama lesson if it is not working for either you or the children but do try to work out with them why it is not working. You are co-participants and often children (particularly those used to drama) will have pertinent insights for you.

If possible involve the children themselves in analysing and evaluating the lesson so that together you can try it again with greater understanding and share the delight of finding you can make it work. Try asking the children some of the questions in Figure 5.1, page 58.

Bringing the lesson to a close

Work towards a dramatic, meaningful and reflective closing moment and don't just break the drama by saying, 'We had better stop now.' Try to end with the children still highly engaged, reflective and wanting more. Maybe the lesson is one of a series or a free-standing lesson; but either way it is important to try to draw the lesson to a dramatic and usually reflective close

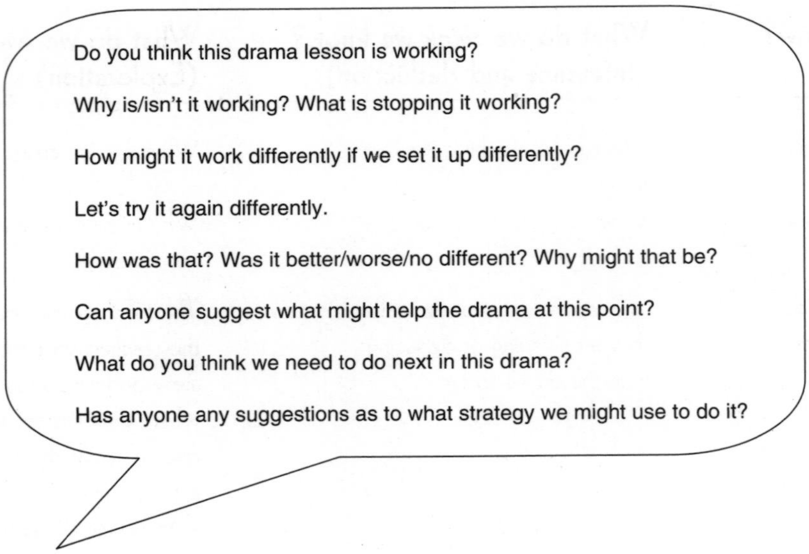

Do you think this drama lesson is working?

Why is/isn't it working? What is stopping it working?

How might it work differently if we set it up differently?

Let's try it again differently.

How was that? Was it better/worse/no different? Why might that be?

Can anyone suggest what might help the drama at this point?

What do you think we need to do next in this drama?

Has anyone any suggestions as to what strategy we might use to do it?

Figure 5.1

rather than just stop it abruptly. It may be that the lesson ends on a cliffhanger but they can find ways of calmly reflecting on it. Avoid letting children leave the drama lesson 'hyped up' and in a state of high excitement.

In what ways can I support the children's reflection at the end of the lesson?

- *Teacher narration with guided visualization*: characters lying down still and dreaming in role at the end can be quite useful! The teacher can use a calming narrative to talk the drama session to a close, 'And as they slept that night, they dreamed silently about what had happened and of what might still be to come … '.

- *Still image with thought-tracking*: holding a moment still and listening to in-role thoughts (thought-tracking) at the end of the session can hold the moment reflectively and then be repeated next lesson as an effective way back into the same place in the drama.

- *Drawing or writing in role*: sometimes asking a character to write a real or imaginary sentence in role or to draw a real or imaginary picture at the end (linked to the drama) focuses and calms, and encourages reflection. If there are characters in the story who are children, then asking them to draw a picture as that child leads to very interesting perceptions being shared visually.

- *Still image and Performance Carousel*: asking the children to create a statue shape that depicts a key past moment or an emotion evoked during the lesson encourages reflection and stillness, while holding engagement with the drama. These can then slowly be formed and melted together simultaneously or in turn, once or repeatedly (and maybe to a calming musical soundtrack).

What about children as audience?

Children need to learn what is expected of them as an audience. Being an audience involves giving the performers your full attention. This applies whether they are an audience in a theatre or an audience within a class drama situation.

Tell those performing:

- They must respect the audience.

- Do not to start your performance until you know you have the full attention of the audience.

- Make sure as performers that you can be seen and heard clearly by the audience.

- You must always do your best for an audience.

- You cannot demand an audience's attention and then not give them your absolute best.

Tell those in the audience:

- They must respect the actors.

- They must give their full attention.

- They must not be distracting to each other and to the performers.

Involving an audience

In drama in education lessons it is possible to give the audience a particular task that attaches to a specific need to pay great attention to the group performance that they may be watching within the lesson, for example:

- Watch this group performance carefully because afterwards you will be asked to speak out loud the possible thoughts of one of the characters from the scene.

- Watch this group performance carefully because they will repeat it twice and the second time will be without sound and one of you will be asked to provide a narrative to go with the scene.

- Watch this scene carefully because at the end of it you may have the opportunity to enter as a new character arriving.

- Watch carefully because in a moment you will be asked to tell the performers two things you particularly like about the their performance, and why, and one thing that you think can be improved, and how.

We do not always have to think of an audience as sitting facing the actors who perform at the front. When children are preparing a scene to perform in a drama lesson it is worth asking them to consider where they will want their audience to be and what instructions they will give to the audience, for example:

- We would like the audience to sit in the middle facing outwards. We will be performing around the outside of the audience because ...

- We want the audience to close their eyes until they hear this sound because ...

- We want the audience to move around the hall with us because ...

- We want the audience to stand/sit all around the edge of the hall because ...

- We want the audience to sit on the floor and leave spaces that we can pass between because ...

- We want the audience to wait outside and all come in quietly together because ...

Of course, children may perform outside their lessons to a wide range of audiences including peers, younger and older classes, parents, community, other schools, and so on. They may need to take account of the physical and cognitive accessibility of their performance to different audiences. There is value in both devising performances with particular audiences in mind as well as creating performances and then later deciding who to invite.

T HE DRAMA UNITS

The units of work above can each be split into several drama lessons. Teachers will want to work through them at their own pace and in ways that best fit the school's own curriculum.

The ages specified for each lesson are no more than a guide. There is no reason why you should stick rigidly to using the lessons only with the year groups suggested.

You can select individual activities from the units. It is not necessary to carry out every activity. You might add activities of your own.

The strategies and conventions used can be readily adapted and transferred to other lessons of your own.

There are cross-curricular suggestions at the end of each lesson. You will need to decide whether you want to intersperse any of these activities with the drama or wait until after the drama.

Unit 1: Visiting Storyland
(Reception and Year 1, ages 4–6 years)

Background information

This lesson sets up a way of taking a whole class of young children into an imaginary drama world together and back again safely. Once the children have experienced this lesson, the same techniques and rituals can be used again to visit any imaginary drama world, for example, under the sea, an unknown planet, another time or place in history, inside a known storyworld from a book or film, and so on.

Resources

Access to an instrument to use as a signal, for example, tambourine. You may wish to use atmospheric music as a background when the children are exploring in Storyland but it is not necessary.

Unit 1: Visiting Storyland

Activity	Purpose/s	Drama strategy	Teacher guidance
1) **Class circle (seated)** Tell the children that you will all be *pretending* to visit Storyland together. Say that there are parts of Storyland we know about because we have already read about these places and the people who live there in story books or been told stories about them. But today we will be visiting part of Storyland where the stories have not even been made yet. We will not find characters and places we already know. We might meet characters living there who no one has ever met yet.	• To set an expectation that the children will be creative not just recall and recount what they already know	***Teacher in Role*** (co-participant)	Young children will immediately start asking questions or telling you information that is personally rooted and not always relevant to all. Do not spend too long responding to hosts of individual responses at the start of the lesson as you need to get all the children 'drama active' early and get the whole class to Storyland. But pick up on any insecurities about going and make sure they realize it is pretend and you are going with them. You could say that to get to Storyland together you all have to leave at just the right moment, which is very soon, but that there will be plenty of time to talk together once you all get there.
2) **Class circle (seated)** Ask if any of them have been to any part of Storyland before. What was it like? What was the most interesting/exciting/beautiful thing they came across? Usually there are plenty of suggestions but if not, say that even if they have not been before they may have dreamed about it or heard rumours about it. Listen briefly to their ideas. Ask what they are expecting/hoping to see there.	• To build up a shared fictional setting, build up anticipation and support the less imaginative children through idea-sharing	***Teacher in Role*** (co-participant)	You can join in and say what you have seen/imagined is in Storyland but let the children's ideas come first or they will mostly imitate you. If their ideas are not forthcoming then you may need to offer some.

(Continued)

Unit 1: Visiting Storyland (Continued)

Activity	Purpose/s	Drama strategy	Teacher guidance
3) **Class circle (standing)** Tell them its time to go to Storyland but unfortunately you cannot remember how to get there. You know there are three things that have to be done by everyone all together but cannot remember what they are. Can any of them remember? If not, do they have any suggestions?	• Raising the status of the children and lowering that of the teacher • Offering ownership to the children	***Teacher in Role*** (co-participant)	You are feigning amnesia! This lets the children help you out. If they struggle for ideas you can vaguely remember, for example, 'I know there was something we had to do with our hands. What might that have been?'
Enthusiastically accept the first three manageable suggestions and weave them into a ritual that you clearly sequence, for example, 'Oh yes, that's right. Well done! I remember now we sprinkle story-dust (imaginary) on our heads and then we all hold hands in a circle and close our eyes. That's right. Then we say something all together and step into Storyland with our eyes still closed. Don't open your eyes again until I tell you to or we won't all arrive together.'	• Modelling a narrative • Building dramatic tension through rehearsal of ritual	***Teacher as Narrator***	You may need to enact this with them first as a practice before carrying out the agreed ritual together and entering Storyland.
	• This sets up an agreed ritual that can be used time and again to enter a fictional drama world	*Ritual*	You may wish to re-enact the stages of the ritual together before doing it once more 'for real'. The children will have rehearsed and so know they can carry it out successfully.
4) **Class circle (standing, facing inwards)** Carry out the ritual that has been agreed with the children. Remind them not to open their eyes until you tell them to (which could be through an agreed sound signal).	• To make actions and words have significance for all	*Ritual*	Make sure that the children do not rush straight off to explore.
Class circle (facing outwards) You will need to signal the arrival through your speech also, for example, 'Amazing! Open your eyes. We have arrived. Wow ... look over there! That looks like a river of rainbow colours in the distance. Stand where you are and just have a good look around you first. What can you see? Tell the people near you what you can see.'	• To keep all children within the same shared fiction • To support the visualisation of the imaginary place	***Teacher Narrative***	Pick up and support the children's ideas too, for example, if a child says they can see a castle say, 'Oh yes, I can see it too but not very clearly. Can you describe it for us please?' When the children are telling each other their ideas you might listen and observe or you may decide to join in and partner a particular child.

Unit 1: Visiting Storyland

Activity	Purpose/s	Drama strategy	Teacher guidance
5) Tell the children that they will be able to go off and explore this part of Storyland in pairs. Remind them that as they journey, they will not meet characters and places they already know from books and films. Everything will be new to them. Ask them to decide with their partner in which direction they will go first. Before they set off, remind them that they should return to the circle (walking not running ... maybe in slow motion) as soon as they hear your clapping (or instrumental) signal. Demonstrate the signal.	• To support a partner in role • Introducing a control signal	***Working in Role*** ***Ritual***	Stay alert to pairs that that may require support in deciding where they will go or where one child is dominating. You may wish to stress that they both need to offer suggestions, listen and be heard.
6) Let the children explore Storyland together freely in pairs for just a few minutes.	• To give time and space for the children to actively explore and generate ideas together	***Improvisation***	You can move among them in role, asking questions, eliciting descriptions, gathering information about what they are imagining, passing Storyland information between pairs, adding further stimulus if required.
7) **Class circle** Use the agreed sound signal to call them back in a controlled way. When they are all back, ask them to tell everyone what they have seen. You might support them to link up their ideas, for example, one child finds a footprint and another finds a talking tree. Does the tree know whose footprint it is? Then tell them that they can go off and explore again for a few minutes, until they hear the 'come back' signal.	• Keeping all children within the same imaginary, shared environment • Encouraging interaction and co-operation • Provides an opportunity to pick up and explore the ideas shared by others	***Ritual*** ***Teacher in Role*** ***Improvisation*** ***Improvisation***	The children are usually full of ideas after even a few minutes of improvised exploration. Bringing them back to share ideas and adventures and then letting them set off to explore further feeds their ongoing exploration. Some children return to carry on with their original exploration, whereas others go elsewhere once they have listened to other pairs' adventures. Listening to and accepting all ideas, the teacher can raise the status/self-esteem of particular children through the way she/he responds to their particular contributions.

(Continued)

65

Unit 1:   Visiting Storyland *(Continued)*

Activity	Purpose/s	Drama strategy	Teacher guidance
8) Introduce a problem to be solved. An idea for a problem may have already arisen through the children's improvisations but if none has you can introduce one, for example:	• To build tension and introduce a problem to be solved collectively in a drama context	***Working in Role***	The drama provides a shared imperative for solving a problem together. The problem-solving activity is real even if the situation is pretend.
• An inhabitant of Storyland arrives (teacher in role) and asks for their help to find a lost key. If/when the key is found the inhabitant will reward them by taking them to the door that it opens. What/who might be on the other side of the door?	• Sets up a new drama environment possibility • Sets up a 'never go with strangers' possible discussion	***Teacher in Role***	The problem-solving can be carried out as a whole-class activity or maybe by groups of children (or pairs) coming up with suggestions for the whole-class to hear and consider.
• An inhabitant of Storyland arrives (teacher in role) and is upset because he/she has been bullied by Bullybags. He/she enlists the support of the children about how best to deal with Bullybags.	• Sets up an opportunity to explore anti-bullying actions and discussion, and assess understanding of bullying	***Teacher in Role***	Alert teachers will learn much from the children's contributions about bullying. Try to resolve the issue in the fictional world and after the drama (not during it) you can link the drama bullying to their real lives if you wish.

Unit 1: Visiting Storyland

Activity	Purpose/s	Drama strategy	Teacher guidance
• The Storyland guard arrives (teacher in role) and reports that a new story has been stolen by the Storythief without the King of Storyland having heard the story first. This is against the law. Can the children help him find the story? Maybe they can tell the King some stories to give the Storyguard time to find the thief. Maybe they will set out with the guard to find the thief and explain to him why he must come back and give the story to the King. Maybe they hear the story being told by the Storythief and have to remember it and tell it to the King (possibly by recording it in some way).	• Sets up a discussion opportunity about authorship and ownership • Sets up a drama context for storytelling and recording	*Teacher in Role*	You can encourage the children to ask you questions about the King, the thief and the laws of Storyland, and answer them in role. Just answer a few questions. Pretending to be a bit absent minded or cautious about speaking to them can work well. Do not give masses of information, just snippets that keep them wanting to know more.
9) **Class circle (standing, facing inwards)** To leave Storyland gather the children back into the whole-class circle and tell them that it is time to leave and can anyone remember what you did to arrive safely in Storyland because you cannot quite remember what needs to be done to go back again. Usually the children suggest reversing the three ritual actions carried out to get there. Again agree the ritual using three ideas from the children, maybe rehearse them once and then carry them out together to return.	• This clearly delineates being in a fictional place and back in the classroom, separating the pretend and the real • It gives ownership of the ritual to the children • It provides a ritual that can be used time and again to leave a fictional world behind	*Ritual*	It is important that children know when they are pretending and when not. A clear ritual for entering and for leaving a whole-class drama helps young children particularly to separate fictional and real. With young children you may need to be very explicit. 'We have stopped pretending now and we are not in Storyland any more … but we can still remember it and maybe pretend to visit it again together one day.' Talking with them about Storyland out of role can help them reflect on and make sense of the drama experience.

Possible cross-curricular links

Geography

Making a collective pictorial map of Storyland (a basic one before visiting showing just a few features and adding to it after the exploratory visit). It can be looked at before each further visit and added to again after each visit.

English

Maybe every child who visits Storyland comes back with a story to tell as a gift from the King.

Labelling the pictorial map.

You can take any real or pretend book with you to Storyland and that is the story you wil end up inside when you get there.

Writing letters together to characters that they met there.

Creating postcards of Storyland (they can draw the landscape or a character on the blank side of a plain postcard).

Telling someone who was not in Storyland what happened there.

The children can receive a letter (or invitation) from a character in Storyland and reply to it.

The children could make 'Storyland' passports for their next visit.

Citizenship

Make up the laws of Storyland that apply especially to visitors, for example, 'Drop no litter', 'Steal no stories.'

Art

The children stood in an outward-facing circle and looked around. This can form the basis of a cyclorama to which they all contribute what they see and that are all stuck together to form a 360-degree view.

Unit 2: Billy's Bucket
(Year 1, ages 5–6 years)

Background information

This drama is based on the picture book, *Billy's Bucket*. It is not essential to have the book to hand but it is preferable, partly as it would then integrate reading, writing, speaking and listening (as the National Curriculum requires). If you have the book, then you can read it in parts and stop at the appropriate pages to carry out the activities. However, you can do the drama without access to the book, by using the following story outline and lesson plan. The plan can be divided into a series of lessons. It divides easily into three main parts: getting the bucket, exploring an imaginary underwater world inside the bucket and dealing with a whale in the street. You will notice similarities between this drama and the 'Visiting Storyland' drama. This is to support continuity and progression, moving from using just their existing knowledge of story to using a picture book but in a familiar way.

The idea of the Bully Fish is not in the book and of course through drama you can use the story in the book as a starting point and context to support whatever it is you want to teach. You are not just acting out an existing story; you are using an existing story; bringing it alive and elaborating it, using it actively to create other stories and to help children learn memorably and with enjoyment.

Resources

Having the picture book is recommended (but is not essential). *Billy's Bucket* by Kes Gray and Gary Parsons, ISBN 0-370-32596-6, published by Bodley Head (2003).
You could use a real bucket and a real whelk shell (but an imaginary bucket and/or shell will do).

Billy has a birthday and persuades his parents to let him have a bucket as a present. The bucket turns out to be a special one that contains an underwater world Billy can see. When his dad borrows the bucket without Billy's permission (to wash the car), a live whale ends up out of the bucket and stranded in the street. The problem of the whale in the book is solved by using emergency services to get it back into the bucket. In the drama we enter the story in role and extend it. We go into the underwater world to explore with Billy, meet objects and characters that we create and talk to, and find ways to help solve the problem of the whale in the street. The bucket becomes a ritual way of the class entering a shared fictitious world. The same imaginary bucket can be used in other lessons to enter and create other fictitious worlds and environments. It can become a repeated device that young children will become familiar with as a way of entering a drama. Effectively, a bucket can become a 'drama bucket' or a 'story bucket' that we enter in role, to go to other places and times together.

Resource sheet 2.1:   Picture of the whale in the street

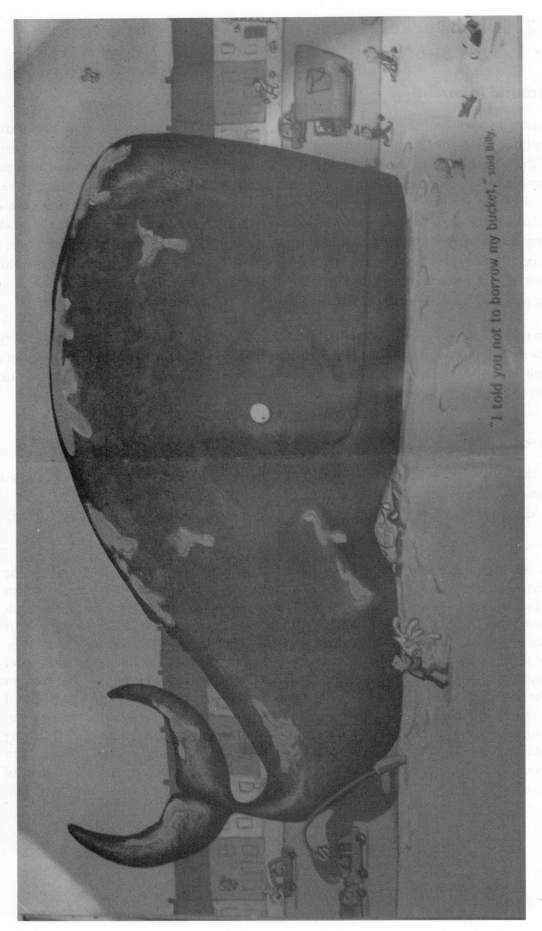

Unit 2: Billy's Bucket

Activity	Purpose/s	Drama strategy	Teacher guidance
1) **Class circle (seated, including teacher)** Tell the children that you are going to pretend to be Billy. His birthday is soon. He wants a bucket but his parents are trying to persuade him to have something else. Tell them they will all be Billy's mum or dad and should work hard to persuade you (Billy) to have a different present. They should offer persuasive reasons, for example, not just 'Have a bike' but 'Have a bike because …', 'Have a new computer because …'.	• To encourage persuasive speech	*Teacher in Role*	Listen to each suggestion and welcome it but give a reason why you do not want what is being suggested, for example, 'But I like my old bike because the saddle is really comfy' and 'I don't want a new computer because I'm used to the one I've got'. Receive and respond to various suggestions before letting them know those contained in the book.
Now you can read this part of the book aloud and add the children's ideas to the existing narrative (as if their ideas are written in the book), so that they hear their ideas coming back to them through your storytelling/reading.	• To extend the text	*Collective Role*	Children like hearing their ideas being used as this signals that their ideas are valued and that it is worth offering ideas.
	• To model how the children's ideas can become part of the story	*Teacher as Storyteller/Teacher Narrative*	
2) **Class circle (standing)** Tell the children that Billy's parents took him to a bucket shop with many different types of buckets on display (Buckets R Us). Ask them to close their eyes, stand with legs a little apart, feet flat and imagine they are a bucket! Each bucket thinks it is the best in the shop. Ask them to keep their eyes closed and imagine that they can see themselves, as a bucket. You might say:	• To engage with role through creating images in the mind	*Working in Role (as objects)*	Most young children will close their eyes if requested but a few feel insecure about it and you should not insist they do.
	• To engage with role through making it physical	*Physical Theatre*	Make sure that the children are not sitting too closely together. If they touch each other with eyes closed at this point, it will break their concentration.

(Continued)

Unit 2: Billy's Bucket (Continued)

Activity	Purpose/s	Drama strategy	Teacher guidance
'You think you are the best bucket. I wonder what you are made of? ... Are you plastic, metal or some other material? ... What colour are you I wonder? ... What would it feel like to pick you up? ... What is your handle made of? ... How is it joined? ... Are you heavy or light to carry? Do you have markings or patterns or pictures on you ... or are you plain? ... What does it feel like to touch you? Why do you think you are the best bucket? What would you say to someone if you wanted them to buy you?' Make sure you pause between each question to allow thinking and visualization time.		*Guided Visualization*	The pauses are necessary for the children to have time to think and respond to your questions in their visualizations. Do not bombard them with the questions. You may find it helpful to close your own eyes and do the activity too, as this helps you with timing your questions.
3) **Pairs (while standing in a class circle)** Now ask the children to turn to the nearest person. They are now a pair of buckets in a shop full of buckets (Buckets R Us) and they both think they are the best bucket in the shop. They are going to have a conversation with each other and try to come out as 'top bucket' (bucket brinkmanship). They can only use speech and cannot touch each other.	• To deepen role engagement through dialogue • To enable a rehearsal without audience before performing	*Improvisation* *Talking Objects*	You may need to partner a child if you have odd numbers in the class. It is necessary to ban touch for this activity as the dialogue could take a confrontational turn and children should be challenged to deal with possible conflict verbally rather than physically.
4) **Pairs (while standing in a class circle)** Tell the children that you will walk around the outside of the circle. As you are nearest to each pair, this will be their opportunity to repeat their conversation as buckets, loud enough for everyone to hear. We all want to hear snippets of what each pair of the buckets have been saying to each other. You will only stand by each pair long enough for them to speak a few sentences, before you move on.	• To enable all children to be heard working in role, by an audience • To build up the shared, imagined environment of the shop	*Eavesdropping (overheard conversation)* *Talking Objects*	You passing around the outside rather than the inside of the circle means all pairs can see and be seen. You need to sense when to move on to the next pair. If you take too long with each pair, then the activity will become overlong and the rest of the class might get bored (which can lead to misbehaviour and disengagement with role). If you hardly stay by each pair at all, then the activity loses its purpose and listening becomes tokenistic.

72

Unit 2: Billy's Bucket

Activity	Purpose/s	Drama strategy	Teacher guidance
5) **Class circle (standing)** The children stay as buckets and you pass by them as Billy this time. They have the opportunity to try to persuade you to buy them. As Billy, you can reply to them but move on. Billy is looking for one particular bucket and none of them are it.	• To give an engaging context for persuasive speech to be spoken and heard	***Teacher in Role*** ***Talking Objects (Physical Theatre)*** ***Improvisation***	You need to listen appreciatively to what they say as buckets and yet reject them without being critical. You can appreciate their fine points but explain you are seeking one particular bucket, even though they too are great buckets!
6) **Class circle (seated on floor)** Tell the children that you will now become a shop assistant. Would any of them like to join you in the middle of the circle (the performance space) as Billy's mum or dad? Accept a pair of volunteers (or up to four children if you wish, as they can share the roles). Explain that Billy has seen the bucket he wants and it is very high up on a shelf. They need to persuade you to get it for him. You can play the role in any way you wish but try to not be too accommodating. Make them really work at getting you to climb a ladder to get the bucket. You might offer a bucket you claim is identical, or tell them that the assistant that is allowed to climb the ladder is at lunch, the manager is out too, you cannot climb the ladder without the manager on premises, and so on.	• To offer an improvised performance opportunity with audience • To present problem solving opportunities in role • To practise talking with shop assistants	***Teacher in Role*** ***Small Group Improvisation***	If you just respond straight away by getting the bucket for Billy's parents, then there is less dramatic interest or tension than if you resist getting the bucket he wants for a while. Without being unpleasant or rude as a shop assistant, you can be fairly unhelpful.
It may be interesting to freeze the scene and while your co-actors (Billy's parents) are stuck in a freeze-frame, you alone can step out of the scene and appeal to the audience in some way, for example, 'I am only refusing really because I am frightened of heights. I lied at the interview for this job and said I could climb ladders. What shall I do? Help me please'.	• To give opportunity for audience interaction with/direction of a character • To show that our first assumptions about people may be incorrect	***Forum Theatre***	Stepping in and out of the scene as a character and talking with the audience is a version of forum theatre that enables the audience to speak with the character and maybe influence his/her speech and actions before he/she steps back into the scene. Sometimes the character can pass over the role to a member of the audience, for example, 'Would you like to come into the scene now as the shopkeeper instead of me, and take over the role (or 'rewind' and play it differently)?'

(Continued)

Activity	Purpose/s	Drama strategy	Teacher guidance
7) **Class circle (seated on floor)** As Billy you fill an imaginary bucket with water, sit in the circle with the children and look into the bucket excitedly. Say, 'Wow!' as if you have seen something amazing inside it, then say, for example, 'In Billy's bucket there was a shark with snappy teeth'. Then pass the imaginary bucket around the circle and use repeated speech all together with everyone saying each time, *'In Billy's bucket there was ...'* and then individual children in turn having opportunity to add their own idea, for example: ALL *'In Billy's bucket there was ...'* CHILD *'... a treasure chest with gold in it.'*	• To give every child the opportunity to contribute to and build a shared, imaginary environment • To use a repeated speech activity/game in the context of a drama	***Teacher in Role*** *Mime* *Drama Game* *Ritual*	Try to ensure that children offer some description of what they see. If a child simply says 'In Billy's bucket there was an octopus', ask more to encourage and elicit extended speech and thought, for example, What does it look like? What is it doing?
8) **Class circle (seated on floor)** It may be that someone has already said (during previous activity) that there is a mermaid in the bucket. If not, you could add this information. Tell the children that you will enter the centre as a mermaid and that they will be able to talk to you but that you (as mermaid) will not talk to them for very long. Then enter the circle and sit pretending to sob. The children will no doubt begin to ask you questions, for example, 'Why are you crying?' 'Can we help you?' and so on. As the mermaid, tell them in response that you are in a cave hiding from the Bully Fish. You are frightened of him. He has chased you and called you names and you ran away and ripped your beautiful tail on a rock. Your mermaid sisters all swam off in different directions and you are now alone and frightened to go back outside the cave and home to the underwater castle where your dad, the mer-king, is.	• To encourage curiosity and questioning • To encourage sympathy and empathy • To give opportunity for collective problem solving • To address the issue of bullying and how to tackle it (using role to safely give a distance).	***Teacher in Role*** *Hot-seating*	You could have a different character being bullied other than a mermaid, that is, another living character children offered during Activity 7. You can, of course, make up a different story to tell as the victim, and possibly tailor it to an issue that is really happening in your school. If you choose to do this you must stay firmly in role as the character, and not make the links too explicit to the children until after the lesson or suddenly drop the role and speak as teacher. If you are using drama to deal with a real incident, you should work in parallel. You are not a psychodramatist! Role gives a safe distance to explore real issues but the drama is a fiction. It may draw on what is real for content ideas but ethically cannot blur real and pretend (causing confusion about if we are in or out of role) during the drama itself.

Unit 2:   Billy's Bucket

Activity	Purpose/s	Drama strategy	Teacher guidance
9) **Class circle (standing)** Tell the children that the inside of the circle is still the inside of the bucket. You will all be going inside the bucket together. There are several (about three) actions that you need to do together to get into the underwater world safely but you cannot remember what they are. Can they offer suggestions? Accept with thanks, a small number of manageable suggestions and rehearse carrying them out together in sequence. For example, all hold hands in a circle together, close eyes, count to three and step over the edge, keep your eyes closed until I tell you to open them. We need to open them together to make sure we all arrive in the same place'. Rehearse the actions once and then do them, 'for real'.	• To shift teacher/ pupil status and empower the children as those with the knowledge • To require inclusion and to stimulate in every child a sense of belonging to the class	*Ritual*	Do not insist young children close their eyes, invite them to. Some are insecure about closing them in public so do not make an issue of it. You can, of course, say and add whatever you wish to get all the class carrying out a simple ritual that gets them into an imaginary place together at the same moment. Do not make the ritual too long or complicated or you will create anxiety in some children about remembering and lose their engagement with the role and fiction. The rehearsal makes them more secure about being able to do the short ritual, as they rehearse being successful.
On arrival, signal you have all arrived, for example, 'We're here. How wonderful. Don't go anywhere yet though, just stand still and take a good look at what is around you. Talk with someone next to you about what you can see and where you might go to explore'.	• To enable them to experience how simple actions can have dramatic significance		
Gather from the children some of their ideas about what they can 'see' and where they might explore with a partner.	• To build a shared vision of the imaginary setting	*Paired Improvisation*	
10) **Free use of space** Tell the children that they can go off with a partner to explore anywhere in this underwater world together. They do not need to worry about the Bully Fish as he is asleep and will be for several hours. Before they set off in role together agree a signal that means, 'come back in slow	• To ease anxiety of children who find reality and fiction difficult to separate • To ensure controlled and safe movement	*Paired Improvisation* *Ritual*	It is unlikely that you will have children seriously concerned about meeting the Bully Fish but you can pre-empt this by saying he (or she) is asleep. Also it prevents immediate high action drama at a time when you want them to explore and create their own places and events within the drama.

(Continued)

Activity	Purpose/s	Drama strategy	Teacher guidance
motion' (maybe a distinctive and repeatable hand clapping percussive rhythm).	• To enable sharing of ideas that might influence others' actions		
Let them explore together freely for a few minutes before signalling their return. Then let some pairs tell the whole class briefly, in role, what they have seen and done, and answer a few questions.			
Then let them go off once more and explore for a few minutes more (maybe to places they have now heard about) before signalling their final return to the class circle.	• To allow creativity but within one overall fiction	*Paired Improvisation*	
11) **Class circle (standing)** Tell the children that they cannot take back objects from this underwater world as the objects do not belong to them, so they should put on the floor anything they have taken.	• To raise awareness of ownership and theft		Usually they will have picked up pretend objects to keep. You could have an interesting discussion later about whether or not it is alright to keep what is not yours in a 'pretend' drama? Naturally this gives opportunity to deal also with real-life theft.
Say that it's time to go back out of the bucket and ask them to suggest what you all need to do to get out together at the same time. They may suggest reversing how they entered the bucket or offer different ideas. Carry out a few manageable suggestions and transport them back in the way they suggest.	• To reinforce that simple actions can have dramatic significance	*Ritual*	
12) **Class circle (seated)** Say you will now be Billy again. Ask them to guard your bucket as you have to go to bed. They should not let your mum or dad borrow it as it's your special bucket.	• To challenge the children into justifying and explaining	*Collective Role*	Although the responsibility for guarding the bucket is imaginary, the feeling of responsibility will be real.
Place the bucket ceremoniously in the centre of the circle and then re-enter first as Billy's mum and then as his dad. As mum you want to use the bucket to water your roses. As dad you want to wash the car.			

Unit 2: Billy's Bucket

Activity	Purpose/s	Drama strategy	Teacher guidance
Listen and respond to the children's appeals and protests as you try to justify taking the bucket, for example, 'Billy will never know if you don't tell him', 'I paid for the bucket so I can borrow it if I want to', 'Billy would let me borrow it if he was awake', 'I would lend my bucket to Billy if I had one, so it's fair if I borrow his', and so on. Do not manage to take the bucket away with them watching as it will create confrontation and chaos. Ask them to close their eyes and narrate the following as a way of getting the bucket: *'The children looked after Billy's bucket but after a while they felt very tired and fell fast asleep ...'* Then wake them up as Billy. Pretend to be looking out of the window ... *'Oh no! Dad must have borrowed my bucket to wash the car. Now there is a big whale in the middle of the road. Oh dear! Dad's car is squashed and he looks very angry.' ...* You could show them the picture in the book now (Resource sheet 2.1) or you can create your own description of the scene, that is, barking dog, bent lamp post, shocked woman with pushchair, car accident as the driver was distracted, neighbours looking out of windows, man dropping a paintpot from the top of a ladder, and so on.	• To see whether the children will challenge you in role with confidence	*Improvisation*	It will be interesting to see if the children are able and comfortable about challenging you in role. It could be an indicator of their level of engagement with the fiction. They can do in a 'pretend' what they might feel unable to do usually.
	• To move the narrative on to a key incident	*Teacher as Storyteller/Teacher Narrative*	Do not blame them for the bucket going missing. Focus them on the scene in the street.
	• To stimulate a tableau • To support a visualization		
13) **Within a big class circle (seated)** Explain that you will all be taking it in turns to enter the circle and stand very still as someone in the picture. They can add new people to the scene that are not in the picture already. In turn they should enter, say who they are in the	• To support gradual engagement with role	*Freeze-frame/Tableau*	

(Continued)

Unit 2: Billy's Bucket (Continued)

Activity	Purpose/s	Drama strategy	Teacher guidance
picture and offer a little information before freezing in position, for example:			You can ask the children to suggest and add in other characters and events to the scene in the street that are not in the book. You can say that we see part of the scene in the picture but there are also people and happenings just outside the picture that they can create.
'I am the man standing at the top of the ladder and I have just dropped my paint.'	• To engage with a new role verbally		
'I am the lady with the pushchair and my child is very frightened of the whale.'			
Gradually the still scene (tableau) will be created.		*Tableau*	In the tableau insist that they are still and quiet except as they contribute their entry sentence. The atmosphere will be very different if they fidget and chat and would lose its theatrical impact.
Then tell the children that when you click your fingers the scene will come alive for a while. Before clicking your fingers, narrate the following:	• To ensure the same starting moment for the action		
'In the middle of the street was an enormous whale gasping for breath. Cars were beeping their horns, babies were crying, dogs were barking and everyone was amazed …',	• To set the scene	*Teacher Narrative*	
Let the scene run spontaneously for a few minutes before freezing it again.		*Improvisation Freeze-frame*	When they are all improvising, you could join in rather than watch.
14) **Free use of space** Say to the children that a newspaper reporter will be arriving (you in role) and then restart the scene and enter as the reporter, asking them who you need to speak to in order to get the story for your newspaper. Interview the characters in the scene, for example, Billy's dad, Billy, driver in accident, and so on.	• To give them a focus for reporting	*Teacher in Role*	Before you start interviewing get the children to tell you the people you most need to talk to and why, for example, Billy's dad because he took the bucket, and the man who has had the car accident as it is a serious incident.

Unit 2: Billy's Bucket

Activity	Purpose/s	Drama strategy	Teacher guidance
15) **Groups of about four** Tell the children that the problem of the whale in the street was solved. You do not know how but they do! In groups of four they need to create and show a possible solution to the whale problem, as a still image (as if it was a photo that appeared with the story in the newspaper). As a press photographer you could then take digital or imaginary photos of their still images in turn. They can also make up a sentence caption that could appear with the picture.	• To give an engaging context for group problem-solving • To give a reason to communicate a plan visually • To encourage discussion and synthesizing of ideas	***Working in Role*** ***Still Image***	Telling the children that they have the solution and you do not know what it is stops them from seeking a 'right answer' and, instead, sets them thinking about a range of possible solutions and alternative endings. You could see each group's solution in turn and let the class ask supportive questions about each plan.

Possible cross-curricular links

Geography

A large circle of paper could represent the bottom of the bucket and they could create together a pictorial map of the bottom of the seabed before or after the visit.

Other circular maps of different environments could be created with some pictorial details and the same drama activities used to enter the world they portray, for example, an island, a forest.

English

You could create Billy's birthday invitations, the newspaper report about the incident, a letter to a friend about the whale incident, signs found in Buckets R Us, a notice Billy put on his bucket afterwards.

Create possible missing pages in the book, for example, additional pages of possible birthday presents, additional pages for the whale scene with a reporter included, other pages of things Billy sees inside the bucket, the children inside the bucket exploring, and so on.

Mathematics

When the shop assistant climbs up the ladder, it can be used as an opportunity to count aloud together in different intervals, for example, counting up and back in 1s, 2s, 5s, 10s. Effectively the ladder could become a number line.

The bucket is one among many rows and columns of buckets. This could give an opportunity for linking simple co-ordinate work.

The bucket shop gives an opportunity for buying and selling buckets of different prices and getting change.

Art and Design

Create additional pictures for the book, based on the drama and draw and paint them in the same style as the artist, Garry Parsons.

Tell the storydrama as a series of drawn images (maybe as a zig-zag book or storyboard).

Create a picture of the seabed with pop-up flaps that cover sea creatures and treasures.

Science

Some of the materials buckets can be made of are mentioned in the book, for example, rubber, plastic, metal. This can lead to learning why different types of bucket are made of different materials and what the properties of the different materials are. Which bucket would last longest?

Habitats: What creatures live in the sea? Why can't we breathe in the sea? Could the sea creatures live in tap water?

Design and Technology

The children could design and make a bucket. You could require it to hold water and this could link to science work, finding out first whether different materials available are waterproof or not.

Unit 3: The Great Fire of London
(Year 2, ages 6–7 years)

Background information

This unit of work is linked to the Key Stage 1 National Curriculum for history. The Great Fire is action packed as an historical event and the drama is intended to help children consider some key moments from a human as well as a factual perspective. The diary of Samuel Pepys gives us a powerful primary source of information from which to build a drama, and paintings and prints of the fire, by artists of the time, are also a very good source to underpin and support the drama. The issues and difficulties explored in the drama are some of those faced by the people of London at the time of the fire.

London in 1666

London in the 1660s was overcrowded, had narrow streets, many with timber buildings that leaned towards each other, and was very smelly. Six hundred thousand people lived there and there were no public toilets. Sheep and cows were taken through the streets to market at Smithfield, leaving droppings. Rats were everywhere and were a serious problem and spread much disease. The air was smoke-filled as many people were using sea coal from Newcastle, and on foggy days it was thick smog. The streets were busy from dawn with markets and small shops in people's houses. London was very noisy with the sounds of cart wheels, street cries, barking dogs, and so on. Most streets were unlit at night, although main streets had lantern light until 10 p.m. 'Link boys' stood on some street corners with torches and lanterns, and would light the way for payment. Timber was the most used building material and straw was used on floors and stored in outbuildings.

The Great Fire

In the early hours of 2 September 1666 a fire broke out in the king's bakery in Pudding Lane. Thomas Farrinor (the baker) had a journeyman staying that night, who first discovered the fire around 2 a.m. The baker, his wife and daughter and one servant escaped via the roof, but another maid was killed in the fire. It spread quickly. It had been a hot summer and the wood, wattle and daub in the crowded buildings were dry. A strong easterly wind fanned the flames. Many buildings contained easily combustible materials, such as straw, tallow, hemp, tar, oil and pitch. There was no official fire brigade and local people had to deal with fires using leather and wooden buckets filled with water, and use staves to beat the flames. Iron fire hooks, axes and ropes were used when it was necessary to create firebreaks by pulling down buildings in the path of the fire. People streamed out of the city, mostly with just what they could carry. Any carts and boats available were soon full and rose to exorbitant hire prices. The fire lasted four days and nights and King Charles made his brother, the Duke of York, responsible for preventing looting. Samuel Pepys, the diarist, recorded the event in detail.

Resources

There are many good websites about the Great Fire of London that provide images, documents and associated information (see page 87 for an example).
Resource sheet 3.1 Print of seventeenth-century London street scene
Resource sheet 3.2 Painting of the Great Fire of London
Resource sheet 3.3 Sentence 'facts' about the fire
Resource sheet 3.4 Excerpts from Samuel Pepys' diary

Resource sheet 3.1:   Print of seventeenth-century London street scene

Resource sheet 3.2:   Painting of the Great Fire of London

Resource sheet 3.3:   Sentence 'facts' about the fire

Fish Street is almost burned down.

London Bridge is on fire.

People are jumping into the river.

It started in Pudding Lane.

The ferrymen are just taking only rich passengers across the river.

The fire is on both sides of the river now.

The baker's maid is dead from the fire.

Pigeons are dropping from the sky with burned wings.

Some people won't leave their houses.

Even the stone churches are burning.

The riverbank and the steps down to the river are full of people with their belongings.

Some people say the French started this fire on purpose.

They are knocking down whole rows of houses to stop the fire.

No one can hire a cart or boat now. They are all full.

This strong wind from the east is spreading the fire fast.

Resource sheet 3.4:   Excerpts from Samuel Pepys' diary

September 2nd 1666

By and by Jane comes and tells me that she hears 300 houses have been burned down tonight by the fire we saw, and that it is now burning down all Fish Street, by London Bridge. So … I walked to the Tower and there got up upon one of the high places … and there I did see the houses at the end of the bridge all on fire, and an infinite great fire on this and the other side … of the bridge.

… the Lieutenant of the Tower tells me that it began this morning in the King's baker's house in Pudding Lane, and that it hath burned St. Magnus Church and most part of Fish Street already. So I rode down the waterside … and there saw a lamentable fire …

Everybody endeavouring to remove their goods, and flinging into the river or bringing them into lighters that lay off; poor people staying in their houses as long as till the very fire touched them, and then running into boats, or clambering from one pair of stairs by the waterside to another. And among other things, the poor pigeons … hovered about the windows and the balconies, till they some of them burned their wings and fell down.

Having … seen the fire rage every way and nobody to my sight endeavouring to quench it … I went next to Whitehall … word was carried to the king … I did tell the King and Duke of York what I saw … and the King commanded me to go to my Lord Mayor from him and command him to spare no houses.

I hurried to St. Paul's; and there walked along Watling Street, as well as I could, every creature coming away laden with goods to save and, here and there, sick people carried away in beds. Extraordinary goods carried in carts and on backs …

At last I met my Lord Mayor in Cannon Street … he cried, 'Lord, what can I do? I am spent: people will not obey me. I have been pulling down houses but the fire overtakes us faster than we can do it.'

February 28th 1667 (almost 6 months later)

… it is strange to think how to this very day I cannot sleep a-night without great terrors of fire …

Unit 3: The Great Fire of London

Activity	Purpose/s	Drama strategy	Teacher guidance
1) **Class circle (seated)** Show an image of a London street in the seventeenth century (Resource sheet 3.1). Tell them that the streets were very busy, noisy and smelly. Ask them to travel the picture using an ear first, that is, if they were standing in the picture, what might they hear? Give all the opportunity to say, 'I can hear…' and complete the sentence, for example, 'I can hear a dog barking', 'I can hear people chatting', and so on. The sounds can refer to things that are not visible in the picture, but could possibly have been heard, for example, 'I can hear church bells', 'I can hear cart wheels on the cobbles'. Repeat this activity using a nose, 'I can smell …', for example, 'I can smell dog mess', 'I can smell bread baking'.	• To encourage a multi-sensory response to the picture • To start engagement with role and setting	*Working in Role*	You may find it helps if the children already have learned a little about seventeenth-century London streets and buildings before starting the drama. This is not essential but it could help them engage more securely and easily with an historical drama. If suggestions are made that do not fit historically you will need to decide whether to deal with this at the time, or come back to it after the drama lesson, for example, the sound of an aeroplane. You need to make sure that what is historically authentic is not lost through keeping the drama going.
What might people be doing in the street on an ordinary day in 1666? Gather suggestions, for example, shovelling animal mess, loading a cart, selling meat, holding horses, herding sheep or cows to market, hanging washing out, carrying shopping home, selling sea coal, and so on. Accept all possible ideas and be prepared to offer more ideas.	• To assess prior knowledge and learning		You might find out about authentic jobs and occupations with the children before the lesson. You could have them listed and ask children to select one rather than try to guess at jobs.
Using the space individually or in pairs Tell them that they will pretend to be people living in London in 1666. Ask them to decide on an activity that they will be doing on an ordinary day there and then make a still image of themselves doing that activity. You may need to offer activity suggestions. They can work alone or in pairs.	• To engage with different roles	*Occupational Mime* *Still Image*	Move among the children and be in role yourself. Interact with them in role, as this helps them engage with their roles, helps you learn about their thinking and signals that you are a committed co-participant.
Explain that when you click your fingers, the scene will come to life and they can move and talk in role. Storytell the scene before clicking your fingers.	• To ensure a clear start to the scene	*Occupational Mime/ Improvisation*	Make sure that you create a dramatic and atmospheric beginning when you narrate. Do not just read and throw away the lines. Use the suggested narrative as a starting point but feel able to create more narrative if you wish, feeding in what you want the children to know and maybe feeding back through the narrative ideas you have picked up from their roles.

Unit 3: The Great Fire of London *(Continued)*

Activity	Purpose/s	Drama strategy	Teacher guidance
It is September 1st in the year of our Lord, 1666. The streets of London, where we live, are crowded, noisy and stinking. Rats scuttle amongst the rubbish. It has been a hot summer and it is going to be another hot day in this overcrowded city … (then click fingers to signal the start of the action).	• To create the dramatic setting and build atmosphere • To model storytelling	*Teacher Narration*	
Join in as a fellow Londoner, asking questions of them and maybe buying their goods and services.	• To deepen children's engagement with role	*Teacher in Role*	
2) **Whole class standing (about a metre away from each other)** Tell them that they are still the same roles. The streets are full of rumours and there is a strong smell of smoke. Give each child a sentence strip cut from Resource sheet 3.3. This sentence is the information that they will now pass on verbally to others. Ask them to move around and spread the information to each other as rumours. They can respond to and question each other in role. They can add information of their own, for example: *'Pigeons are dropping from the sky with burned wings.'* *'Have you seen any fall?'* *'Yes. I was almost hit by one that fell near me!'*	• To create dramatic tension • To mix rumour and fact in order to learn through separating it later	*Rumours*	Take part in this activity and use it as a way of feeding in information. You are likely to end up with rumour and fact mixed up. You will need to make sure that the children end up being clear what is based on evidence and what is pure invention. This can be done after the drama lesson or during it. Checking what is true or not can be a research activity afterwards. You could consider with them what has been said to each other that is true, what could possibly be true and what could not be true.
3) **Whole class in long line side by side** There was no effective fire brigade. Explain to the children that they will be forming a human chain that will pass buckets of water along the row from the river to the fire and back again. They can talk if they want but the work is hard. Get them working together passing the imaginary buckets along the line and then you could add in certain information gradually, for example, you need to do this faster, the buckets seem to be getting heavier, your shoulders are hurting now, and so on.	• To encourage whole-class co-operation and a sense of belonging • To make memorable a historical fact (human chains)	*Co-operative Mime*	You could spend some time talking with the children about what the problems might have been with a human chain firefighting by passing buckets of water, for example, spilling it, slower people in the line.

Unit 3: The Great Fire of London

Activity	Purpose/s	Drama strategy	Teacher guidance
You could add to this activity by telling the children that as they pass along an imaginary bucket they could say aloud what they are thinking, for example, 'This is hopeless', 'I want to stop doing this and run away'.	• To enable a personal in-role response to be shared	*Thought-tracking*	You may wish to teach directly before, or after the lesson about the way that the fire was fought then as opposed to nowadays. How did people firefight then and how do we do it now? How do we know how they fought the fire? (sources of historical evidence). You may link this with a visit to a fire station or a museum at some point.
4) **Pairs or groups of three or four** Tell them that the fire is heading this way and that they have just got time to get to their homes and gather a few possessions. They will need to decide with their partner or group, exactly what they will take (that is, only what they can carry without a cart or boat). Will they take or leave animals? Do they have elderly relatives or young children to carry possessions for too? Will they need to carry a child? What is the one personal possession that they most want to take with them?	• To give a dramatic context requiring reasoning, justifying and evaluating decisions together	*Improvisation*	You will need to decide if they can work effectively in groups of three or four, or whether they need to do this activity in pairs. Working in pairs is less challenging than in groups of four. Do not let them gather more than they could carry. The idea is to consider the value of particular objects to them during a crisis. What *must* they take (if anything)? What would they take if they could? What can easily be left? It is worth considering with them why they have selected certain objects rather than others. Are their choices to do with monetary value, sentimental value or survival?
Ask them to pretend to collect whatever belongings they have decided to take and then make a still image of them leaving and shutting the door of their home for the last time.	• To hold their focus on a significant moment	*Still Image*	
Each child then should have opportunity to speak aloud the thoughts and feelings of their character at this moment, that is, 'The moment I left my home for the last time I thought/felt ...'. You can ask each pair or group to stay still in their images and individuals just speak their in role thoughts/feelings aloud as you pass by them in turn.	• To encourage empathy	*Thought-tracking*	
5) **Pairs or groups of three or four** Pepys' diary is full of incidents he was eye witness to (Resource sheet 3.4). There are also well-known paintings and etchings which show us what it must have looked like (Resource sheet 3.2).	• To use authentic historical sources to inform and shape the drama		The Internet has many educational sites that have images and text linked to the Great Fire of London that could be useful here. For example, the picture used in the lesson is (on page 82) available at http://www.molg.org.uk/English/NewsRoom/Archived07/RelightsGreatFire. htm

(Continued)

Unit 3: The Great Fire of London *(Continued)*

Activity	Purpose/s	Drama strategy	Teacher guidance
Ask the children to imagine that they were there and saw some of these sights as they journeyed away from their homes. They can also make up sights that could have been seen. Gather their ideas and maybe remind the children again of some of the things Pepys and others reported, for example, burning warehouses on the riverside, poor people refusing to leave their homes, looting, people in human chains passing buckets of water, pulling down buildings to make a firebreak, packed boats on the Thames, London Bridge burning, a man killed when he went into a church to get a blanket, a live cat with all fur singed away, burnt birds in the streets, people walking across rooftops, falling down cellars, over-laden carts, people guarding their possessions at the riverside, sick people being carried on beds, people carrying musical instruments and other valued possessions.	• To encourage creative responses • To encourage active engagement with historical documents		A linked museum visit would be very stimulating and helpful. The diary language of Pepys (Resource sheet 3.4) is interesting for the children to read and hear but may need to be translated into plain English to be fully understood. You will need to make sure they understand unfamiliar vocabulary such as 'looting' and decide what is too sensitive for your class. You could explain that even though massive things were happening during the fire, such as houses being pulled down, important smaller things were happening too, for example, a burned dead bird falling. Children may find it easier to engage with this incident rather than an action packed scene, as it is closer to their real-life experiences of dead birds. Also, often 'less is more' in performance (one of the reasons for making the performance short and focused).
In pairs or groups of up to four ask them to make up and act out a very short scene (no longer than a minute) of something that Pepys did see or might have seen during the fire.	• To enable them to demonstrate their knowledge and understanding of events	*Improvisation* *Small Group Play-making*	
Ask the pairs and groups to get into a long, horseshoe-shaped line, so they can all see each other and you can journey as Pepys, moving along from one group to another. Tell them you will walk close by each scene in turn and it will come to life when you are nearest to it and then freeze when you move away. Only the group you are standing nearest to can move or make sound and others need to be still and silent like an audience.	• To bring together parts of the drama, link and share them (thus staying in one overall drama)	*Performance Carousel* *Teacher in Role* *Eavesdropping*	Insist on a theatrical atmosphere throughout the performances. Remind them that they need to able to hear and see each other and an audience must give all their attention and be very still and quiet. You could ask them to play the scenes a second time and interact with them a little as Pepys, with the children improvising their responses.

Unit 3: The Great Fire of London

Activity	Drama strategy	Purpose/s	Teacher guidance
6) **Pairs** Some people refused to leave their homes. Ask for suggestions as to why this might be, for example, denial, unable to move through fear, not willing to leave their possessions unguarded, hoping the fire will change course, and so on. Select from among these pairs activities, maybe adding other ideas of your own (or the children's own ideas). You might decide they can try several in turn. Tell the children that:			You can create other possible scenarios that are suitable for children to improvise in pairs. The ideas can be connected to Pepys' diary or pictures and other primary sources. An Internet search will yield paintings, etchings and documented accounts of the fire that could be studied and stimulate other possible improvisations in pairs or small groups.
• One of them refuses to leave their home and the partner will have to work hard at persuading them they should. They can use only words to persuade and reason and may not use any physical contact or force.	*Improvisation*	• To give a context for using persuasive speech	You could pass amongst the working pairs and join in alongside a character, for example, you too could try to persuade someone to leave their home. This gives you the opportunity to model persuasive speech and to collaborate with one of the children.
• One partner wants to leave but is simply too frightened of heights to step out onto the roof (which is by now the only means of escaping the fire). The other partner must try hard to coax the other to step out onto the roof. This time some supportive (but not forceful) physical contact can be offered.	***Teacher in Role (optional)***	• To give a context for justifying, communicating and reasoning	
• They have both just left their house as the fire is coming but one partner wants to go back into the house to get a blanket. The other needs to dissuade her/him from re-entering the house. No physical force may be used.	***Improvisation in Pairs***	• To encourage empathy and an appreciation of the viewpoints of others	You will of course need to take account of the fact that the fire has gruesome stories associated with it and your children are very young. You have the advantage that they are creating the scenes and so they are in their control and that drama is working at a distance through role.
• One person is leading a team that has come to pull down your house to create a firebreak. The other person is the house owner who does not want them to.			

(Continued)

Unit 3: The Great Fire of London (Continued)

Activity	Purpose/s	Drama strategy	Teacher guidance
Following the improvisation, explain to the children that you will now pass by each pair in turn. Everyone needs to be still and quiet. When you are standing next to a pair they can come to life in role and be heard by everyone.	• To create a moral dilemma • To give opportunity for every person to be heard by all and the fiction to be shared	*Eavesdropping*	Nonetheless, stay alert to any aspects of this lesson that may resonate strongly and personally for a particular child, for example, they may have had experience of a real fire or an eviction. Always be prepared to adapt or stop the drama, come out of role and deal with any necessary real concerns that arise. You have the opportunity to linger longer by some pairs. Insist that those who are not performing give their complete attention as audience to the pair who are performing.
7) **Pairs or groups of up to four** Ideally look with the children at the painting of people at the edge of the Thames (Resource sheet 3.2). Encourage observation and discussion about the painting. Tell the children that many people made their way down to the riverside. Ask why people might have headed for the river? (For example, ferry boats, water they can use if necessary, and so on.)	• To use an authentic visual stimulus to stimulate discussion and inform the drama	*Still Image*	Make sure that you praise them when they demonstrate good drama skills, for example, 'Well done. You were really still then ... as still as a picture'. This is an opportunity for them to be made aware that paintings can depict real and/or imaginary events and people, and to consider why there are no photographs of the Fire of London.
Ask the children in groups to imagine that they are a group of two, three or four Londoners who made their way together to the riverbank and ended up being painted later by an artist who was also there. Ask them to make a still image of their pair or group as they finally appeared in the artist's painting. They need to know who they all are pretending to be and what they are actually doing at the time.	• To support engagement with a role • To help them make the connection between the painting and real people in the past		

Unit 3:   The Great Fire of London

Activity	Purpose/s	Drama strategy	Teacher guidance
Then a group at a time will come to a line defined by the teacher (the river's edge) and add themselves to a long, life-sized painting of the scene. This should be done as performance, with the pairs and groups making their way to the scene in a controlled way, as if entering a stage (that is, they enter as actors would, rather than as themselves). As groups enter in turn and add themselves to the tableau, suitable background music could be used as an atmospheric addition (optional).	• To slow down the building of the whole scene to enable the children to gradually process information • To make the construction of the tableau itself a theatrical experience	*Tableau*	Try to ensure they walk to and enter the tableau in role. If you use music it helps connect the whole tableau.
You will then narrate the scene to life and all groups simultaneously will start to improvise for a short time (no more than a minute) following your narration and an agreed signal, for example, finger click. You can make up your own narrative or use the following: *'On the banks of the River Thames were a heaving mass of frightened people of all sorts and ages, huddled around and guarding their few remaining belongings, desperately hoping they could escape the fire. Rich and poor shoulder to shoulder with the same thought – survival. The river was littered with boats of all types and sizes. Most were already more than fully loaded and were dangerously low in the water. They were filled full with possessions and people, mostly those people rich enough to pay enormous amounts of money to the ferrymen. The smell of smoke, the sound of fire and fear and sights that would haunt these people's dreams forever … '(signal to start).*	• To give authentic information as narrative, yet theatrically • To ensure the scenes come alive at the same moment	*Improvisation* *Teacher Narration*	Use your narration to focus attention on and add significance to the tableau. You can weave the children's work into the narrative, for example, if one group is depicting someone stealing its goods, then you can make reference to it in your narration.

(Continued)

Unit 3: The Great Fire of London *(Continued)*

Activity	Purpose/s	Drama strategy	Teacher guidance
Pepys records in his diary that he is still troubled by dreams of the fire, months later. Tell the children that not many people were actually killed in the Fire of London and that they have all survived but, like Pepys, still dream about it. Dreams are often exaggerated rather than realistic. Also some dreams can be repeated. Ask the children to work in pairs or groups of three or four and create a very short dream about the fire or create a dream that has big, slow motion movements. You might consider adding the additional challenge that the dream sequence should be repeated twice continuously.	• To encourage reflection on the drama and its events and characters	*Mime and Movement*	This activity may well require you to talk a little about dreams with the children. How are dreams different from real life? How are they the same as real life? Why do they think Pepys kept dreaming about the fire? What types of dreams do they have? What makes us remember some dreams more than others?
Using performance carousel (see Activity 5) ask the children to perform their dreams in turn. Try to set it up so that as one group's performance ends, the next one starts seamlessly.	• To bring the drama to a controlled and reflective close	*Performance Carousel*	We need to remember that dreams are revealing but can depict hopes and fears and not always lived experience.

Possible cross-curricular links

History

How do we know about the Great Fire of London (diaries, documents, paintings, and so on)? If the children went to London now, what buildings would still be there that preceded the fire? If there was a fire in London now, how would it be put out differently by firefighters? How did people hear about a fire then (word of mouth, bells) and how would they hear about it if it happened now (alarms, media)? Why are there no photographs or films of the Fire of London? Why can we not really talk to someone who saw the fire?

English

There are opportunities for further diary writing in role as Pepys. The drama created by the children will have incidents and scenes that can be reported in diary form. Telling incidents and scenes in role to another person first, before writing them, will support the writing process. Other reasons to write in other genres can arise from the drama, for example, a letter afterwards to a relative, poetry written about the fire or as the fire! The writing activities could be done as shared writing rather than individually.

Art

The Fire of London was depicted by many artists and it would be interesting to study and compare paintings, etchings, and so on. What different scenes have been represented? What was used to do the picture, for example, oil paints, wood engraving, pen and ink and so on? The children could be introduced to some of these techniques.

The children could paint (individually or in groups) the scene they were part of in the tableau (Activity 7). The paintings can then be gathered together to form a collage of the scene alongside the Thames.

Music

The fire as a theme lends itself to musical composition or to creating a sound effects collage. The children can experiment to find objects and instruments that can be used to depict aspects of fire, for example, sparks, glowing embers, explosions, roaring flames, crackling wood, gushing water (firefighting), and so on. Different groups could take different aspects and then you can help bring them together and conduct them in a symphony of fire. This could be recorded. It could act as a soundtrack for parts of the drama or a fire dance.

Dance

Fire also works well as a theme for movement and dance. The various movements associated with fire can be explored and then combined creatively through improvised or rehearsed dance, for example, spiralling smoke, spreading smoke, wind-blown fire (directions), crackling and sparky, flickering flames, inferno, flames dying down, embers, and so on.

Unit 4: The Drums of Noto Hanto
(Year 3, ages 7–8 years)

Background information

This lesson is based on a true event that took place in 1576 during the Japanese civil war. The event took place on the coast near the village of Nabune, on the Noto Hanto peninsula. The villagers (fishermen and farmers) outwitted armed samurai who were coming to attack them. The villagers made frightening masks and makeshift statues from bark and seaweed, and played loud music on the Taiko (drum) to scare the warriors away. The Taiko drums are used to signal many things and 'war song drumming' (*Gojinjo Taiko*) is said to date back to this event. Taiko means drum in Japanese and these traditional drums have been in use for 3000 years. The drums used to be used to signal village boundaries, give battle commands and to signal danger. Priests used to use Taiko to communicate with gods. In Japan the Taiko is a symbol of purification and was used to get rid of evil spirits. Each year the victory of the Nabune villagers over the samurai warlord, Kenshin, is still commemorated with a festival.

Resources

Several drums and drumsticks are required (at least enough for each group of five children to have a drum).

There is a picture book that can be used to support this lesson but it is not essential to use it. *The Drums of Noto Hanto* by Alison James with illustrations by Tsukushi, ISBN 0-7513-7227-7, published by Dorling Kindersley (2000). If you use this book, do not show the cover until after the drama lesson as it could give too many clues for Activity 5.

The Internet offers interesting images, maps and articles about Noto Hanto and gives its history, including information about a recent earthquake in 2007. Photographs on the Internet mostly show an unchanged landscape that could inform the drama and add atmosphere if projected.
It is not essential to have Japanese Taiko drum music to accompany this lesson but it could provide a relevant soundtrack to enhance parts of the lesson, and can be found and ordered online.

Unit 4:   The Drums of Noto Hanto

Activity	Purpose/s	Drama strategy	Teacher guidance
1) **Standing in a space individually** Tell the class that the Noto Hanto coastline has many jagged rocks that have been weathered into strange and spiky shapes. Ask them to move around the room, keeping in a space and when the drumbeat stops they should make an extraordinary rock shape using their whole bodies.	• To engage with the setting • To increase spatial awareness	*Movement*	Remind them to use different levels and not always make a standing shape. Different body parts might touch the floor apart from feet.
Pair work Repeat this but when the drum stops they should link themselves physically to at least one other person to make a joint 'rock' shape. They can attach in more than one place.	• To break down physical barriers and encourage co-operation	*Physical Theatre/Still Image*	Remind the children that again they can join themselves in different ways and should try to ensure the shape is stable and still.
You could extend this into making one collective whole-class shape that all the children in turn add themselves to. They can attach in more than one place and to more than one person. Real Taiko drum music would be good to use as a soundtrack but is not essential. You can drum the beat.	• To encourage whole-class co-operation and a sense of unity	*Physical Theatre/Still Image* *Tableau*	Again remind them that they should not just make their shapes standing. They should also not just use hands to attach to each other. Emphasize that once they have joined the tableau they need to be completely still.
As you pass by each person in the tableau can they each offer a descriptive word for the landscape, for example, lonely, wild, empty, rugged, and so on.	• To develop a shared vocabulary linked to the setting		You can add adjectives too during this activity to extend their vocabulary.
2) **Class circle (seated)** Tell the class that the drama will be about a true story that happened in Japan, about 500 years ago. They will be pretend to villagers who live in a village called Nabune. There are no cars or electricity, of course, and no other villages close by. The village is on the coast and most people are farmers or fishermen. The people grow rice as the main crop. Ask them to suggest what jobs	• To give authentic information about the drama setting		The children will need some information to start the drama and engage with an appropriate role. They have researched about Nabune and Noto Hanto before the drama lesson. They do not need much information to get the drama started and the drama itself is likely to arouse their curiosity about Nabune.

Unit 4: The Drums of Noto Hanto *(Continued)*

Activity	Purpose/s	Drama strategy	Teacher guidance
people might be doing on an ordinary day there, for example, planting rice, mending boats and nets. Then ask them to get into a space and create a still image of themselves doing a job as a Nabune villager.	• To encourage engagement with the people and place • To start to engage with role	*Working in Role* *Still Image*	If they suggest inappropriate tasks you may need to guide them to others and grasp this as a teaching opportunity.
Individually in a space You will narrate the start of the drama and use a sound, for example, a single drum beat, to signal that they should bring their still images alive and start miming their tasks. Agree a signal that will tell them to freeze again and be very still, maybe another single drum beat or call out, 'Freeze!'	• To prompt the action	*Occupational Mime*	Teacher narrative models storytelling and enables you to introduce whatever language or information you wish to the drama.
Your teacher narrative could be along the lines of ... 'It was early in the morning in the Japanese village of Nabune and the villagers were hard at work (sound signal to start mime) ...'. Move among the villagers and question them about what they are doing and, after you freeze the action, you can narrate further using the children's ideas, for example, 'Fishermen were loading their boats, women were washing clothes in the stream and the farmers were out in the fields planting rice ...'.	• To provide more information about the drama setting and their roles	*Teacher Narrative* *Freeze-frame*	You may be questioning them while they are in role. Once your narrative reflects and uses the children's own ideas, they will be particularly engaged with what you are saying.
Seated in class circle Then tell the children that the villagers use drums (Taiko) to signal important events and happenings in the village. Ask them what sort of events might be signalled by the drums, for example, the birth of a child, the end of the harvest, the arrival of a stranger? Pass a small drum and stick around the circle. Each child in turn will have the opportunity to create one drumbeat sequence and say aloud what it means, for example,	• To make explicit the link between music and ritual	*Ritual*	You might wish to point out that in our culture we use church bells rather than drums to signal, for example, ring in the New Year, wedding peals, and so on. We also have specific music for special events for example weddings, harvest and so on. If children are stuck for an idea then they can just pass the drum on or beat it and pass it on.

Unit 4: The Drums of Noto Hanto

Activity	Purpose/s	Drama strategy	Teacher guidance
'When people get married *we play the drums*' and 'When we have finished planting crops *we play the drums*'. The phrase '*we play the drums*' is repeated each time and can be chorused by everyone. You add, 'When strangers arrive in our village, *we play the drums*'.	• To introduce a drum signal required for the next part of the drama	*Teacher in Role*	You only need to add the signal for a stranger arriving if it has not already been offered by one of the children.
3) **Individually in a space** Explain to the children that they will start their village jobs again and that this time they need to stay alert for drum signals. If they hear a signal that denotes a stranger is arriving, they should move into a village meeting circle and sit. When they are in the middle of their mime, you need to beat the drum to signal that a stranger is arriving. Keep repeating it until they are seated in the circle, ready to meet the stranger.	• Re-entering/engaging with a setting, through repeated mime • Building dramatic tension	*Occupational Mime*	
4) Tell them that you will enter the meeting place as a stranger who wants to talk with them. Arrive confidently and tell them you are the messenger of the greatest warlord, Kenshin. Tell them they should surrender and give their lands to him or he will take them by force very soon. He is on the way already with his warships. You will take their reply back to Kenshin. Tell them that you will be back soon for their answer and move away from the scene. Listen in as teacher. Judge the best moment to go back in again as Kenshin's messenger for their reply. In role, listen to and accept their decision, even if reluctantly, and tell them you must get back to Kenshin and report. If they say they will	• To give important information to move the drama forward • To set up a problem to be solved in role • To encourage debate • To reach a collective decision	*Teacher in Role*	Play the role as a confident but not confrontational intermediary. You are just the messenger, and avoid making them hostile towards you. You may even offer sympathy to avoid hostility. As teacher you want them to explore the problem through debate and agree, if possible, their course of action. Whatever decision they have arrived at you will need to accept. You need to get back to Kenshin. You may tell them they have made a mistake if they refuse to surrender but the decision is theirs. They are unlikely to decide to surrender and are more likely to start hatching plans!

(Continued)

Unit 4:   The Drums of Noto Hanto *(Continued)*

Activity	Purpose/s	Drama strategy	Teacher guidance
surrender, compliment them on a wise decision. If they will not surrender, tell them they are being foolish as Kenshin is so powerful, but then take your leave. If they try to prevent you leaving, 'Freeze' the action and narrate the drama to another time and/or place, for example, 'The villagers were so angry they attacked the messenger but whatever the villagers decided to do to the messenger, it was not going to stop Kenshin from coming ...'.	• To set up a dramatic moment requiring them to communicate a joint decision effectively	*Teacher in Role*	It is unlikely they will prevent the messenger from leaving but, if they do, remember that you have the power to stop the drama or move it in a different direction at any moment.
5) **Groups of no more than four** Tell them that historically the villagers successfully came up with a plan to prevent Kenshin from invading. They did not use weapons, they used very clever thinking and working together.	• Providing authentic historical information		Will you decide which children are in each group this time, or will they? Be alert to avoiding dominant leaders and passive followers. Tell them that good group work lets everyone contribute ideas and be listened to. Move among the groups as they work and if necessary remind them that everyone's ideas must be listened to even if not all ideas are used.
Each group is now going to try to come up with a plan to foil the invasion. They should think a little about what resources the villagers had. They must use cunning and working together, and not use force. Tell them in advance that all the plans will be presented afterwards at a village meeting. So, as well as coming up with the plan, they may need to think about how the group's plan will be presented well to an audience of fellow villagers.	• Raising awareness of the need to prepare presentations and the benefits of doing so	*Working in Role*	Remind them that, if they are presenting, they need to be clearly seen and heard and may need to practise projecting their voices without shouting.

Unit 4: The Drums of Noto Hanto

Activity	Purpose/s	Drama strategy	Teacher guidance
6) **Whole-class circle** Ask each group in turn to present their plan and then enable constructive questioning of each group by the rest of the villagers. You might be able to suggest that there are parts of different groups' plans that could be linked together to create one village plan that all will have contributed to. Co-operating rather than competing is likely to strengthen the plan.	• To encourage co-operative teamworking • An opportunity for peer support • To practise communicating clearly to an audience	*Performance* *Questioning in Role*	Ensure that the children ask genuine questions and in ways that are positively framed. Sometimes children ask questions that are a way of putting down another's ideas. They need to be coached to ask questions that genuinely support each other's thinking. They might consider, 'Why am I asking this question? Do I want to know the answer? Am I asking it in a way that is sensitive to the person I am asking?'
At this point it is possible to take the lesson in different directions. You could enable them to enact their group plans through a series of three linked still images that show the plan in action (culminating in showing them in turn through a performance carousel – each group performing in turn without pausing between groups) *or you can return the drama to what the villagers actually did do* (Activity 7) and draw out any parallels with the children's own ideas.	• To synthesize the plan into key images • To quickly create a continuous whole-class performance	*Still Image Sequencing (Image Theatre)* *Performance Carousel*	
7) Tell the children that their plans might well have worked. What the villagers actually did was frighten the samurais' ships away by making and wearing big frightening masks and giant puppet sculptures with scary faces. They played the biggest Taiko drums very loudly (war drumming) and terrified the approaching warriors who retreated. They made the masks and sculptures from natural, 'found' materials, for example, seaweed, bark, twigs, shells, and so on.	• To give authentic information about an historic event		It will be necessary at some point during or after the drama to ensure that the children have the 'real' historical version of this event. When you are doing anything historical in drama there must be a respect for evidence and the fiction must not end up mixed with fact after the lesson is over.

(Continued)

Unit 4: The Drums of Noto Hanto (*Continued*)

Activity	Purpose/s	Drama strategy	Teacher guidance
Groups of five With one drum per group of five, each group will devise a scary group dance. It should be a dance with a repeated movement sequence (not chaotic, random free movement) and each group will be performing their dance twice through to the rest of the class. One person is the drummer. The drumming also needs to be a repeated sequence and not just random loud drumming.	• To give opportunity for devising/creating a group dance that is visual, auditory, kinaesthetic and maybe tactile	*Movement/Dance*	This activity has restrictions placed on it to get the children to move beyond just making disorganised unchoreographed movement and spontaneous sound. The challenge of having restrictions to work within can actually stimulate higher-quality creative thinking than being given total freedom to devise.
Divide the class into two, so that half the groups will be performing to the other half of the class. Remind the performers (villagers) they are trying to scare the audience (warriors). The audience can stand as if they are on the side of a ship and should remain speechless while watching the spectacle. Once the performance is over, they can respond by speaking their in-role thoughts aloud in turn, for example, 'Are these humans or spirits?' 'Will it be safe to land?' 'We should turn back!' You could also gather the in-role thoughts of the performers, for example, 'Will this work?' 'I am frightened', 'This is our only hope', and so on. Swap over so that all will have a turn at being both dancers and warriors.	• To evoke a specific emotion within an audience • To share in-role thinking and encourage inter-thinking • To cognitively and affectively experience different viewpoints	*Movement/Dance* *Thought-tracking*	This is a controlled way of handling half the class making a lot of noise and 'frightening' the other half. The drama gives a tight structure for the experience and enables it to become effective theatre as a means of emotionally and cognitively engaging with the situation, rather than allowing a potentially chaotic improvisation that would lack value and result in the dramatic tension falling apart. It would not be sensible to allow ongoing chaotic dance and would disturb other classes and get drama a bad name!
8) **Sitting or standing in pairs** Ask the children to get into pairs and label themselves A and B. Then you select from the following pairs of roles. 1. A young Nabune child (A) being told of the event by a parent who was involved (B)	• To calm the children down and encourage reflection	*Improvisation*	You could create other pairs of roles or the children could. It may be worth discussing with the children (maybe after the drama lesson) what makes a good storyteller and what makes a good listener. Good listening is active not passive. A good listener gives their full attention and may then question well, without interrupting.

Unit 4:   The Drums of Noto Hanto

Activity	Purpose/s	Drama strategy	Teacher guidance
2. The child of a samurai warrior (A) being told of the event by a parent who was on the ship (B)			
3. A foreign visitor to Nabune (A) being told by a tourist guide nowadays about the event (B)		*Storytelling*	
4. A Japanese visitor to Nabune (A) being told by a Nabune villager (B) about the event a few weeks after it	• To encourage empathy and develop an understanding that events are open to different interpretations by different tellers and listeners		
Do this activity twice so that all children get a chance to be a storyteller and a listener.			
9) **Groups of four** Tell the children that each year the people of Nabune commemorate the victory by holding a festival. Ask the children to create a group movement/dance that could be performed at the festival. It should depict important moments of this true story simply but it is not necessarily to be presented realistically. Some children may feel able to present in a symbolic and/or stylized way, for example, they could make their bodies into a big drum or all move into being one 'monster' on the shore.	• To provide authentic cultural information • To actively encourage group reflection on key aspects of the drama	*Performance*	It is not necessary to perform for an external audience. They can just perform for themselves or each other. It is just that this story is performed annually and so the performance has a particularly meaningful context in relation to the drama.
You can create a festival with the groups' performance pieces in any way you wish. If you decide to create a procession with this activity, tell the children this at the start as it will impact on their devised piece, for example, 'It needs to be a performance that uses travelling movement so that you can perform as you move along together in a class line.'	• To actively consolidate and communicate the learning		If you decide to use this drama as part of a cross-curricular project rather than as a stand-alone drama, then you may well have created masks that can be used. You could link in music making with this in your music lesson maybe, programme and poster design in art and design, and so on.

(Continued)

Unit 4: The Drums of Noto Hanto *(Continued)*

Activity	Purpose/s	Drama strategy	Teacher guidance
• Maybe they will perform this for an external audience, for example, in an assembly using masks.			
• Maybe they will just enjoy performing together in a festive atmosphere at the end of the lesson.			
• They could turn their performances into a festival procession (maybe around the playground) that stops to let groups perform from time to time.			

Possible cross-curricular links

Geography

Locate Noto Hanto on a map. It is a peninsula jutting out into the Sea of Japan. Find other peninsulas.

Discuss ways to get to Japan. Travellers' personal websites about visits to Noto Hanto may be of interest.

English

The ancient Haiku is a Japanese poetry form. Haikus are short, do not rhyme and are focused on one subject. They are usually three lines long and contain up to seventeen syllables. See if the children can create a Haiku based around this historical event or moment they have explored through the drama, for example:

> Warriors approach
>
> Masked men hiding
>
> The weak are strong

History

What are the ways we commemorate important historical events, for example, dance, processions, paintings, poems, stained glass windows, carvings, songs, stamps, and so on?

Use the Internet to explore the history of masks.

Citizenship

In the drama the villagers meet to make a village decision. How are village decisions made in our country? How are national decisions made? If a decision needs to be made in school that effects the children, how can they contribute to the process of decision-making, for example, class or school councils?

Design and technology

Design, make and then use drums. Who can make the drum with the most terrifying sound? The loudest sound? The lowest sound?

Research and create a recipe for sushi and consider why rice, seaweed and fish is staple food in Japan. Make and/or eat sushi if possible.

Science

Link drum sounds to work on the science of sound. How far and fast does sound travel and how? Use drums to explore this out of doors. What happens if the wind or sound or ear is in a different direction? What affects the travel of sound? What would have been the ideal conditions for the sound of the Taiko to travel to the warriors' ships?

Music

Ask them to make drum sequences that a partner listens to and then repeat, or in a class circle take it in turns to make drumming sequences that everyone repeats.

The picture book, *The Drums for Noto Hanto*, records the drumbeat phonically and uses different font sizes to indicate the level of sound. Ask the children to make a drumbeat sequence and record it (maybe phonically) in a way that can be passed on to someone else to play. They may use standard notation or create their own.

Let them listen to drum solos and then create and perform their own. They could listen to a cultural range of drums, for example, different African drums, Japanese, and so on.

Art

Make terrifying masks from natural, found materials.

Create large puppets, using natural and found materials (ideally in a forest or on a beach).

Do some simple origami.

Make pictures of the story by paper-cutting and sticking.

Finding out about the Japanese artist, Tsukushi (who has illustrated the picture book with paper-cut pictures of this story).

Create shadow puppets and scenery to tell the story, using an overhead projector.

Religion/art/drama

Use the Internet to find out about how masks are still made and used in different parts of the world. Are masks used just to entertain? What beliefs do some cultures and religions hold about certain masks?

Unit 5: Environmental Sustainability – 'Don't build it where we live!' (Year 4, ages 8–9 years)

Background information

This lesson is based around an imaginary village situated near the Norfolk Broads and brings alive the universal theme of environmental sustainability and the conflicting feelings and interests of inhabitants, developers, landowners, planners and visitors/holidaymakers. It also raises awareness of the need to consider natural habitats that support wildlife.

An imaginary holiday company have bought riverside land from a local farmer and want to develop it as an environmentally friendly, residential holiday site. This drama can be adapted to be about a different fictitious geographical place that better fits your own local circumstances and curriculum. You can still use this lesson outline and its drama strategies and sequence. But schools also need to study an environment that is beyond their locality, so this lesson may well be directly relevant to the many schools who choose to study the Norfolk Broads.

This unit of work is a further development of a successful series of lessons carried out with several Norfolk schools, who were involved with the Broad Futures* project. The lessons aimed to actively raise awareness of environmental sustainability issues and support children to come up with possible solutions.

Resources

An Ordnance Survey map of the Norfolk Broads
Large sheets of paper (one between four children) and thick felt pens
Some music that could become the soundtrack for a leisure holiday film (optional)
Resource sheet 5.1: A map of the proposed holiday development site at Wranham Broad
Resource sheet 5.2: Key facts about the village of Wranham and the proposed holiday development site
Resource sheet 5.3: Role cards

---

*Thanks to Neil Seal, who helped plan these lessons and trialled them successfully

Resource sheet 5.1: A map of the proposed holiday development site at Wranham Broad

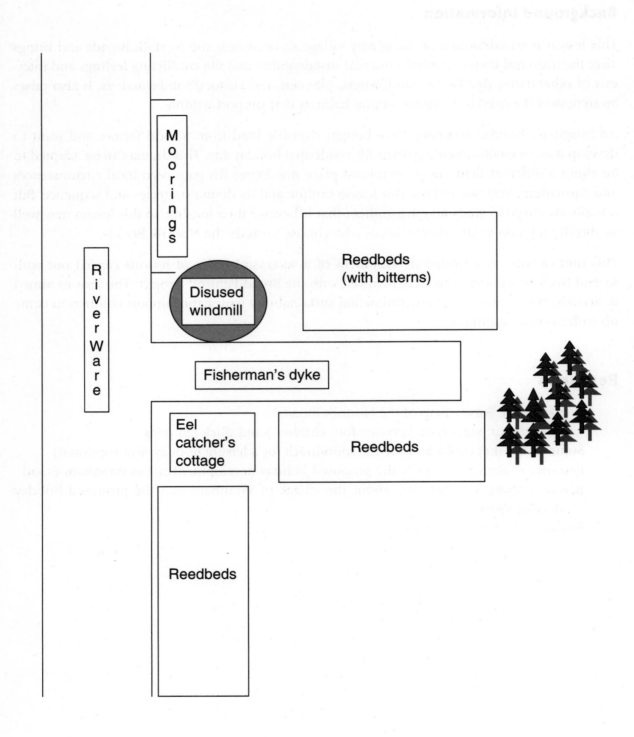

Resource sheet 5.2: Key facts about the village of Wranham and the proposed holiday development site

The birds and butterflies that breed there will need to be protected.

There are two overnight mooring spaces that boats can stay tied up to free for one night only.

Local fishermen can use the river's edge free (apart from their annual licence fee).

The existing bridge is just a footbridge.

The nearest road is a field away.

No one is allowed to swim in the water.

The local pub and shop are not making much money and could close.

It is hard to get council permission to build new houses in the village.

There are few jobs. Most working villagers drive half an hour to the city to work.

Most of the councillors were born in the village and have lived there all their lives.

The windmill and eel catcher's cottage are both in need of repair and are protected buildings, so cannot be pulled down.

Resource sheet 5.3: Role cards

David Bishop
David is a Tourism Officer and wants the development. He has to get as many tourists into Norfolk as he can as they bring in money. He also thinks tourism will create new jobs. He knows that with cheap flights abroad less people have been taking holidays on the Broads.

Mary James
Mary is an ecologist from the local university and does not want the development. She says there are rare plants on the site, on the land and in the water. She also says that there are breeding bitterns on the site and it is a breeding ground for swallowtail butterflies that need to be protected.

Paul Bannister
Paul does not want the development. He has recently retired here after a lifetime of working in London. He is now living in his ideal retirement home and would not have bought it if there was a holiday development nearby. He does not want to move again and thinks the development will make his house worth less and harder to sell.

Clive Postle
Clive does want the development. He is the pub landlord and thinks that holidaymakers will buy pub meals and he will make more money. He does not want the development to be allowed to have a restaurant or café.

Jenny Musters
Jenny is a Waste Minimization Officer and is against the development. It is her job to try to prevent litter. She believes more tourists means more litter. She also says that tourists do not pay Council Tax and it is the locals that end up with the mess and the cost of clearing the rubbish.

Unit 5: Environmental Sustainability

Activity	Purpose/s	Drama strategy	Teacher guidance
1) **Class circle (seated)** Explain to the children that they will first be taking on the roles of experts in this drama. They will be experts at designing holiday centres. You will be entering in role as Jessica Cory, owner of the award winning, 'Waterside Happy Holiday Company'. (WHH) You will be choosing which among these top designers you will employ for an important development job. Tell them that whoever is selected will earn a lot of money for their design. When you enter the circle again, you will be Jessica Cory and the drama will start.	• To provide enough information to get the drama started • To help the children engage with their roles	***Teacher in Role*** ***Mantle of the Expert***	Do not make Jessica Cory into a bad character. It is possible that the children will realize a moral dilemma is developing but you do not want them to turn against WHH or Jessica Cory at the very start of the drama. She wants them to design with environmental sustainability and profit in mind. As professional designers the challenge is to come up with a design that will be acceptable to locals and environmentalists and be appealing to holidaymakers.
'Good morning colleagues. As you know, my name is Jessica Cory and I am the owner of the Waterside Happy Holiday Company or WHH for short. Thank you for applying to work with WHH on this very important holiday development. I need to remind you that the design work you will be involved in is secret at the moment, as we do not want local people finding out what we are planning until the plans are complete. Of course we always expect some local people to object to any new holiday development but we need to be sure that the plan we come up with is very likely to be accepted by the council planning committee before local people get to hear about it. WHH is very aware that this site is beautiful and that there are protected birds and butterfly species living there that you will need to take account of. Are there any questions so far?'		***Teacher in Role***	If children are concerned already about local objections, you can point out that some local people will be delighted with the trade it will bring into the area, for example, shopkeeper, pub landlord, and so on. And, of course, they are the very best designers, so it will be their job to make sure that they come up with a design that local people will find acceptable and will be environmentally friendly. They are very skilled and experienced designers and let them know you are confident they will succeed.

(Continued)

109

Unit 5: Environmental Sustainability *(Continued)*

Activity	Purpose/s	Drama strategy	Teacher guidance
2) **Groups of four (seated at table or with floor space for drawing)** Ask the children to get into teams of four designers and give them big sheets of paper and felt tip pens (unless you wish to use to use computers for this design activity). They could make up a company name for their team.	• To establish a group/team identity	*Teacher in Role*	The competition is an incentive but no single design group will actually win. The final design will be an amalgamation of the good aspects of them all, as we want all groups to succeed through sharing good ideas.
Give them maps of the site (Resource sheet 5.1) and present them with the key facts sheet about the site, village and surrounding area (Resource sheet 5.2). You could also, if you wish, use a real Ordnance Survey map and add in where the imaginary Wranham is. You could show pictures from the Internet or holiday brochures of typical Broads landscape scenes.	• To ensure key information is taken into account during the next task	*Mantle of the Expert*	You may wish to remind them of what constitutes good teamwork before they start, that is, all member's ideas listened to and considered, followed by trying to agree fairly together which ideas to use. You may wish them to carry out the design using paper and pens or a computer-aided design programme. If you wish to keep the
In your own words tell them all groups are competing for the lucrative and prestigious WHH contract. In role as Jessica Cory, explain that they will be working in design teams to try to be selected as the team with the best and most acceptable design for the holiday development. They will need to keep locals, planners, holidaymakers and wildlife happy to get the plan accepted.	• To make the brief and design criteria clear	*Teacher in Role*	pace of the drama going then you will probably choose paper and felt tip pens during the drama lesson. They could always convert and extend the design further using a computer at some other time.
Tell them that there is a council planning meeting soon and so they will need to work quickly (tell them they have exactly 15 minutes for this task).	• To use the drama itself to encourage pace and mirror the impact of real working deadlines		

Activity	Purpose/s	Drama strategy	Teacher guidance
3) **Two groups of four** Ask the groups to pair up. Each group will present their plan to another group and then answer any questions about their plan. The listening group might be another group of designers or you could give them different roles, for example, constructively question as if they are: • a naturalist • the shopkeeper or pub landlord • a village child • a planning official (roads and buildings). Afterwards, ask the groups to decide the three biggest selling points of their plan, that is, what are the three points most likely to make your team plan acceptable to all stakeholders (explain the term) or what are the three aspects of your team plan that you are most proud of?	• To give opportunity for communicating the plan clearly • To give a forum for listening to other people's viewpoints • To encourage constructive challenge • To give a reason to prioritize and justify choices to others	***Mantle of the Expert*** ***Improvisation***	You could just get the groups to present in turn to the rest of the class. However it takes a long time to get to listen to every group in turn in an average-sized class. Presenting to one other group gives opportunity for longer presentations and more dialogue. Having to explain their group's plan and then answer questions about it helps them think more deeply and in more detail, before then selecting its three main selling points.
4) **Groups moving around the room** Spread the plans around the room and, as Jessica Cory, give all groups the opportunity to look at each other's plans. As they travel between plans, they could do so as designers or you could ask each group to look at the plans through the eyes of a particular group of stakeholders (see previous activity). Ask each group to sit with their plan. In turn each group has the opportunity to publicize to the audience their three key selling points.	• To share ideas and find out what other groups have been doing • To imagine and consider possible future objections from stakeholders • To give opportunity to prioritize and synthesize	***Teacher in Role*** ***Improvisation*** ***Mantle of the Expert***	Do not let children 'rubbish' each other's plans. You want the children to look carefully, to comment constructively and to evaluate and support each other's work, not negatively criticize. You can structure individual or group feedback and comment if you wish by suggesting they say two good things about each group's plan and offer one suggestion for improvement.

(Continued)

Unit 5: Environmental Sustainability *(Continued)*

Activity	Purpose/s	Drama strategy	Teacher guidance
Tell them that all the plans are so good that WHH₁ would prefer not to just select one plan and thereby lose many good ideas. Your task now as Jessica Cory is to accept key aspects of each group's plan to negotiate and create one combined super-plan that all teams partly own.	• To avoid rejecting good ideas and creating a sense of team failure • To model the way that ideas can be constructively combined	*Teacher in Role*	We want all children to stay motivated and to succeed. Through this activity there is opportunity to share your and their thinking about what might most beneficially be taken from each plan, and why. Cost and lack of space can be used as the only reason you do not take all ideas. You might find it useful to draw the central rough sketch or plan so that there is a visual focus.
5) **Individuals moving around the room** Tell them that despite the initial planning with the designers being supposedly secret, some news of what is proposed is spreading in the village. The rumours and gossip are a mixture of fact and nonsense. Ask the children to each decide one thing that could be being said in the village. They may decide on something factual or make up a false but plausible rumour. They should then move around among each other spreading and gathering new rumours, as villagers, about the proposed new development.	• To create and gather information about what the villagers are hearing • To practically demonstrate how false rumour and truth easily merge • To raise awareness of the power of the media to manipulate public opinion	*Rumours*	This activity is challenging and entertaining as, of course, the children know, as designers, what is being proposed and so will know false rumours when they hear them but are responding as villagers. It would be possible to have half the class as villagers spreading the rumours and half as designers hearing the rumours. The problem with this is that the designers are not supposed to talk about the plans but a few indiscreet designers could try to dispel rumours and may not be believed anyway.
6) **Groups of four** As Jessica, tell the class as designers that rumours are rife and so WHH wants the designers to make a short advertising trailer film about the proposed holiday development that makes viewers want it. The children will probably have seen similar films advertising activity and leisure breaks.	• Offering a reason within the drama for requiring the next activity • To link drama and media	*Teacher in Role*	Make clear why the film is needed. The rumours are potentially problematic and so a propaganda film extolling the virtues of the development is necessary. Of course, an advertising trailer will paint an idealized picture of the development and as it has not been built it may be computer-generated images they will be pretending to be portraying.
In groups of four they will each make and act out a short piece of film that should take less than a minute to perform. Give each group a different theme focus:	• To set up a structure that enables groups to contribute to a collective drama activity	*Small Group Play-making*	

Unit 5: Environmental Sustainability

Activity	Purpose/s	Drama strategy	Teacher guidance
• bird-spotting • butterfly-spotting • accommodation • fishing • children playing • boating • meeting new friends • organized activities • walking.	• To give opportunity for active engagement with the possible positive impact of the plans		You or the children may have suggestions of your own as to what each different group focus could be for the film, as they have the knowledge about what they have already designed earlier that could be important to show in the film.
All scenes should start with the words, 'Welcome to Waterside Happy Holidays' and finish with, 'Come and find out for yourself.' After they have rehearsed their short scenes ask them to perform them as a performance carousel, that is, each group in turn as one continuous performance, during which the non-performing groups awaiting their turn, are completely still and quiet. If you have suitable background music to play during the performance, it could act as a film soundtrack.	• To make clear the start and finish of each scene • To give a common thread to all scenes to support their being part of the same film	*Performance Carousel*	Of course, you could actually make a real film of these scenes and maybe add text, music, and so on.
7) **Two lines (standing and facing each other)** Make sure there is space for you to walk between the two lines of children. Tell them that the villagers are divided as to whether the development is a good idea, for example, it will provide local jobs, it will disturb wildlife, and so on. Tell them you will pass between the lines as the Chair of the council's planning committee. The children in one line will speak aloud reasons why the council planning committee should approve the development and the other line will speak aloud reasons against it. Each child has an opportunity to speak when you are stood closest to them.	• To encourage and share reasoning • To enable all children equal opportunity to contribute their ideas and reasons • To make clear that councillors need to listen to public opinion	*Conscience Alley* *Teacher in Role*	Make sure that the children speak loud enough for all to hear and not just you. It is a drama skill to speak as if to one person but clearly enough to be heard by all. You could travel through the lines more than once, so that they have an opportunity to offer more than one reason.

(Continued)

Unit 5: Environmental Sustainability (*Continued*)

Activity	Purpose/s	Drama strategy	Teacher guidance
8) **Seated for a meeting** Ask the children to imagine now that this is a council meeting. They will soon be making the decision as to whether to agree planning permission, by voting. Before the council planning committee makes its decision they will be listening to various people who have asked to speak to the meeting. Resource sheet 5.3 has five role cards. Invite five children to volunteer to take on the roles. You can play a role or roles if necessary. In turn, the characters on the cards will speak to the council and explain their viewpoints. The council may ask them questions. They can develop the role beyond the information on the card.	• To present a range of viewpoints • To enable questioning and discussion around a range of viewpoints	*Improvisation*	It would be possible to have several children playing the same role at the same time, that is, a group of children enters as one character with the one viewpoint. This is called collective role. This makes it less demanding on any particular child to take on the role single-handed and shares ownership of the role.
9) **Seated for a meeting** The class are the council (although you can have some as public audience at the meeting and maybe as press). Each councillor has the opportunity to briefly speak their viewpoint before the vote. You may need to help them formalize the proceedings as if it was a real meeting.	• To give everyone equal opportunity to speak	*Improvisation*	It may be that if the class have a class council or you have a school council, that they are more able to conduct these proceedings without your support.
When all have had an opportunity to speak then the vote can be conducted. You will need to decide whether to do this as a show of hands or by paper ballot.	• To provide active experience of a democratic process	*Ritual*	You might decide to record the vote in some way and possibly create a press release.

Possible cross-curricular links

Geography

An Internet search cross-referenced to a large-scale map could reveal real Broads holiday sites and developments. The children might be interested to see what similarities and differences there are between their own plans and real developments. They can also consider where and why real holiday developments might have been sited where they are.

English

The local newspaper may well have received letters to the editor about the proposed development. They can write a letter from a particular viewpoint (of an existing character or someone we did not meet in the drama).

If the plan is passed, they could create a brochure advertising the development.

Design a picture postcard of the finished development and write it from a holidaymaker.

Science

Ask them to research about the swallowtail butterfly and bitterns. Where are they found and what habitats do they require? Why have they become less common?

Unit 6: The Discovery of the Tomb of Tutankhamun (Years 4 and 5, ages 8–10 years)

Background information

This lesson is based on the important and exciting discovery of the tomb of Tutankhamun, by Howard Carter on 4 November 1922. The careful work was finished in February 1932. The tomb was discovered after six 'scanty' seasons of archaeological exploration by Carter's team, in the Valley of the Tombs of the Kings, at the point when Carter was considering abandoning the dig. The dig was being funded by Lord Carnarvon. Carter had chosen a good right-hand man (A.R. Callender). His photographer was Harry Burton. Carter was demanding to work for, capable, clear headed, well organized, bossy, laid down clear rules, inspired loyalty, expected obedience and servitude, did not like to be contradicted, could be moody and hostile, stubborn and self-confident.

Resources

Howard Carter's narrative account of this event is told in *The Discovery of the Tomb of Tutankhamun* by Howard Carter and A.C. Mace, ISBN 0-486-23500-9, published by Dover. Key excerpts taken from his diary are used in the drama and appear as italic text. It may be worth you reading Carter's full dramatic and emotional account of the discovery. Carter's obituary is also a good source of information about his life and character.

Resource sheet 6.1: Key dates and events (1922) based on Carter's diary

Resource sheet 6.2: Sentence strips (Carter's thoughts)

Resource sheet 6.3: Photograph of the antechamber (Plate XV111)

Resource sheet 6.1: Key dates and events (1922) based on Carter's diary

Wednesday, 1 November

Commenced operations in the Valley of the Kings … there were ancient stone huts of the Necropolis workmen … these ancient huts were soon cleared of the rubbish covering them.

Saturday, 4 November

At about 10 a.m. I discovered beneath almost the first hut … the first traces of the entrance of the tomb … the first step of the sunken-staircase.

Sunday, 5 November

… Towards sunset we had cleared down to the level of the 12th step, which was sufficient to expose a large part of the upper portion of a plastered and sealed doorway. Here before us was sufficient evidence to show that it really was an entrance to a tomb, and by the seals, to all outward appearances that it was intact … The seal-impressions suggested that it belonged to somebody of high standing … I refilled the excavation for protection … I returned home and cabled to Lord Carnarvon:

'At last have made wonderful discovery in Valley a magnificent tomb with seals intact recovered same for your arrival congratulations.'

Wednesday, 8 November

Received wireless from Lord C. '… *possibly come soon* …' and later, *'propose arrive Alexandria twentieth* …'.

Monday, 20 November

Lord Carnarvon and Lady Evelyn arrived (Cairo).

Tuesday, 21 November

Callender arrives.

Saturday, 25 November

Opened first door … exposed a completely blocked descending passage … As we cleared the passage we found mixed with the rubble broken potsherds, jar seals, and numerous fragments of small objects; water skins lying on the floor together with alabaster jars, whole and broken, and coloured pottery vases … These were disturbing elements as they pointed towards plundering.

Sunday, 26 November

Open second doorway … came upon a second sealed doorway, which was almost the exact replica of the first … Feverishly we cleared away the remaining last scraps of rubbish on the floor of the passage … we made a tiny breach in the top left-hand corner to see what was beyond. Darkness and the iron testing rod told us that there was empty space … I widened the breach and by means of the candle looked in … the hot air escaping caused the candle to flicker … Lord Carnarvon said to me 'Can you see anything'. I replied to him 'Yes, it is wonderful'.

Resource sheet 6.2 (Unit 6, Activity 3)
Sentence strips (Carter's thoughts)

Carter's thoughts (based on his diaries)

Every step we uncover leads us nearer to knowing.

This may lead to the tomb we have been looking for.

But these steps may not lead to a tomb.

We have been disappointed so many times before.

Maybe it's just an unfinished tomb …

Maybe it's a tomb that has not been used.

Maybe it's a tomb that's been robbed many years ago.

It is nearly sunset. We must work fast.

Is this the top of a doorway?

The doorway has been sealed and plastered.

Surely this must be an undiscovered tomb.

I was *right* all along.

Resource sheet 6.3 (Unit 6, Activity 5)
Photograph of the antechamber (Plate XV111)

Unit 6: The Discovery of the Tomb of Tutankhamun

Activity	Purpose/s	Drama strategy	Teacher guidance
We had now dug in The Valley for several seasons with extremely scanty results and it became a much debated question whether we should continue the work, or try for a more profitable site elsewhere. (Carter)			
1) **Class in two lines, facing each other (standing)** Explain to the class that Carnarvon was considering withdrawing his funding and Carter had to work hard to persuade him not to. Tell the class that you will pretend to be Carnarvon. They will be his thoughts. The dig has been going on for five years already and little has been found. Carter has a strong feeling they will be successful but it has cost Carnarvon a great deal of money. Ask the class to face each other in two lines, with a space for you to walk between the lines as Carnarvon. Explain that they will be 'the voices in his head'. One line will be Carter's voice, trying to persuade Carnarvon to keep paying for the dig. The other line will be voices opposing this, for example, 'Think of all the fine objects you will own if he is successful' or 'He is wasting your money. Stop paying'. Each person has the chance to speak aloud when you (Carnarvon) are standing closest to them.	• To consider and share the pros and cons of a particular course of action • To use logical reasoning • To practise persuasive speech	***Decision Alley (Conscience Alley)*** ***Teacher in Role*** ***Thought-tracking***	You need to move slowly along the line and stand next to each child in turn. Stay in role and do not insist each child contributes, pass on with no comment if they 'clap' to signal you should pass by. You can choose to just listen to each voice, or to respond. You can walk through the lines more than once if you want them to offer further thoughts. It would be helpful if you had explained before the lesson about exactly how good archaeologists work and how repetitive and tedious it can be for much of the time.
Season after season had drawn a blank; we had worked for months at a stretch and found nothing, and only an excavator knows how desperately depressing that can be … (Carter) (Resource sheet 6.1)			

Unit 6: The Discovery of the Tomb of Tutankhamun

Activity	Purpose/s	Drama strategy	Teacher guidance
2) **In pairs (standing)** Ask the children to get into spaces (in pairs) and stand by their tools. They have imaginary hoes, pick axes, sieves, brushes, labels etc. Tell them that they are starting on yet another new section of ground and will not be finding anything. They should work together on the hot, hard, back-breaking work. As they are repetitively working, what are they saying about the relentless Carter behind his back? It is rumoured the money will run out soon. You will pass by them as Carter, getting them to work harder and asking questions maybe. They are subservient and fed up. When you are near them they will be subservient but when you move away they can disclose to each other their true feelings about you and the dig.	• To engage with the tedium and depression of a fruitless dig • To experience how a master/servant and co-worker relationship might feel	*Occupational Mime* *Improvisation* *Teacher in Role*	Make sure they realize that they would not be rude to Carter, even if they might be rude about him. Also point out that he will have had supporters among the excavators as well as critics. Questioning the children helps deepen their engagement with the role and helps generate plot, for example, 'When was the last time you found anything?', 'Have you seen anything that gives you hope of a find yet?', 'Are you sure you are looking carefully enough?' and so on.
Freeze the scene and tell them that you will pass among the pairs as Carter and this time when you are near a group we will hear what they are saying behind his back to each other. Only the pair you are near will move and speak and will freeze silently again as you move away and on to the next pair. *We had almost made up our minds that we were beaten and were preparing to leave The Valley and try our luck elsewhere; and then — hardly had we set hoe to ground in our last despairing effort than we made a discovery that far exceeded our wildest dreams.* (Carter)	• To give opportunity for sharing parts of each pair's scenes to inform and build the narrative	*Eavesdropping* *Freeze-frame*	You might want to recap at this point in the drama/narrative, out of role. What do we *know*? For example, Carnarvon might stop the dig. What do we *think we know*? For example, most excavators do not expect to find anything. What do we *want to know*? For example, will Carnarvon stop the dig? Will Carter find anything?

(Continued)

Unit 6: The Discovery of the Tomb of Tutankhamun (*Continued*)

Activity	Purpose/s	Drama strategy	Teacher guidance
3) Tell them to restart the dig. It is 4 November at just before 10 a.m. A hut has been cleared away and they have been digging beneath where it stood. When the repetitive dig is under way again, call out, 'A step! – come quickly – a step cut into the rock! Maybe this leads to a tomb'. Let the children as excavators improvise for a minute or two around the moment the first step is found and then freeze the action. As you pass by each 'frozen' person in turn, they can say aloud, in role, what they are thinking, for example, 'This might be a dead end!', 'At last!'	• To introduce dramatic focus	*Teacher in Role* *Improvisation* *Freeze-frame* *Thought-tracking*	If the children respond by behaving in a silly way rather than being excited in the role of an excavator, then freeze the action and use your role to guide the behaviour, for example, 'Although the team were excited they had to stay still and not rush to dig deeper. Carter was very strict and self-controlled and they knew that to rush at the site could damage important finds and destroy evidence.'
While the scene is still frozen, take 12 clear steps in a straight line, through the 'frozen' workers, while reading the following narrative script (which is based on authentic text from Carter's diary). Take a dramatic step as you read each sentence.	• To create dramatic and tension	*Teacher in Role*	
Step 1: Every step we uncover leads us nearer to knowing. *Step 2:* This may lead to the tomb we have been looking for. *Step 3:* But these steps may not lead to a tomb. *Step 4:* We have been disappointed so many times before. *Step 5:* Maybe it's just an unfinished tomb. *Step 6:* Maybe it's a tomb that has not been used. *Step 7:* Maybe it's been robbed many years ago. *Step 8:* It is nearly sunset. We must work fast. *Step 9:* Is this the top of a doorway? *Step 10:* The doorway has been sealed and plastered. *Step 11:* Surely this must be an undiscovered tomb. *Step 12:* I was *right* all along.	• To raise awareness through performance of Carter's documented thoughts	*Scripted Performance*	Do not worry about the exact words. You are trying to make this moment dramatic and keep the children focused on a key moment. This stylized approach is theatrical and is a way of not moving on too fast. It symbolizes what actually happened. The men had to resist the urge to just rush on with the excavation.
It would be possible to give the lines above (see Resource sheet 6.2) to the children as a script rather than you speak them all.	• To make Carter's thoughts memorable through visual, auditory		

122

Unit 6: The Discovery of the Tomb of Tutankhamun

Activity	Purpose/s	Drama strategy	Teacher guidance
They could select a line each from Carter's actual account and speak their selected lines when you pass by them as Carter.	and kinaesthetic representation		
Twelve children could physically become the 12 steps as they speak the 12 lines, creating a piece of scripted physical theatre.		*Physical Theatre*	
They have found a 'magnificent tomb' with the seals intact. Carter has it buried from view again while they wait three weeks for Lord Carnarvon to come from England to be present when it is opened.			
What did the team say among themselves during those weeks, as they waited?			
4) **In pairs** Ask the children in pairs to talk together about the find and about Carter. They should try to take opposing views about Carter waiting for Lord Carnarvon to arrive, for example 'He has to wait because Carnarvon is paying for this dig'. 'All this time we have been searching and now he's holding us back.'	• To be aware of varying viewpoints about Carter and his course of action • To enable reflection in role about characters and events	*Improvisation*	There are several ways of approaching this. You may decide that the children need some thinking time before embarking on this improvisation, or you can give that as an option. You could ask them to start straight away spontaneously with no pre-role time for preparation. You could let them talk together out of role first about possible viewpoints before moving into role to enact and speak them. You might also decide whether to allow them to create the scene with action and speech or just speech.
Carnarvon and Lady Evelyn have arrived and Callender (an archaeologist friend of Carter's has also joined the dig) at Carter's request. The workmen re-dig to reveal steps (16 steps now) and then a passage and door. A candle was used to test for foul gas.			You may decide to break the drama for a while to directly teach about the objects (as a history lesson) or you may decide to proceed with the drama and let the children learn about/research the objects after the drama lesson.

(Continued)

Unit 6: The Discovery of the Tomb of Tutankhamun (Continued)

Activity	Purpose/s	Drama strategy	Teacher guidance
... details of the room emerged slowly from the mist, strange animals, statues and gold – everywhere the glint of gold. *Carnarvon:* Can you see anything? *Carter:* Yes, wonderful things.			There are several photographs of the antechamber and its contents to be found in Carter's book. Resource sheet 9 could be projected large (almost like scenery) to help the children imagine they are really looking into the room (antechamber) during this part of the drama.
5) **Groups of four** Project for the class (or give each group) Resource sheet 6.3, photograph of the objects. They were first seen by Carter by a single torchlight. Assign one object to each group. As a group they need to study their one object carefully together, talk about how they would describe it to someone. They may or may not know exactly what the object is.	• To engage with an authentic stimulus	*Physical Theatre*	Move among the groups and support if necessary. Ensure safe touch. They do not need to script much and could repeat the same sentence several times if they wish.
Then ask them to form themselves into that object together physically (four bodies together become one object). They will practise from a lying or crouched position on the floor, growing slowly together into becoming that object. Then they need to hold themselves still as the object for a few seconds before speaking as the object, describing themselves (through performance), for example, 'I am a beautifully carved animal', 'Look at me. I am covered in the finest gold.' They can experiment with speaking in turn and/or together, as the object. They then freeze together silently and slowly return (in unison) to lying or crouching still on the floor.	• To stimulate and encourage group co-operation • To give opportunity for devising/creating a group performance	*Talking Objects* *Freeze-frame*	Encourage them to truly work as a group and listen to and use each other's ideas rather than let one child dominate and others not contribute. Try to pick up on performance skills. • Is there complete still and quiet before the first group starts? • Are their still images absolutely still? • Can the group start and stop at exactly the same moment?
When they have all prepared their performance, tell them that you are Carter with the torch. You will shine it on each group in turn and when it is shining on them it will be their turn to perform. Only then	• To create a unified class performance that gives a sense of being part of a group and a class	*Performance Carousel*	

Unit 6: The Discovery of the Tomb of Tutankhamun

Activity	Purpose/s	Drama strategy	Teacher guidance
will that group start to show their performance. The non-performing groups stay totally still and silent in the shadows. You could join the performance yourself by speaking from Carter's diary, as if you are Carter remembering what you saw and/or conclude it by saying (as Carter wrote): *Surely never before in the whole history of excavation had such an amazing sight been seen … imagine how they appeared to us as we looked upon them from our spyhole in the blocked doorway … the first light that had pierced the chamber for 3000 years …* What did the excavators think and feel as the first people to look upon this sacred scene for 3000 or 4000 years?			• Is the audience completely still and silent as they wait for their turn? • Can speech be clearly heard? You could ask the children to evaluate their own and each other's performances against the above criteria. If you are lucky enough to have a spotlight available and a blackout facility, you could use this very effectively as the wandering torch beam … or you could use a powerful torch and just draw the curtains for atmosphere and theatrical effect.
6) **Same groups of four** Tell them that they will be all getting back into group positions, as the objects in the antechamber. You will pass among them as Carter. As you pass nearby each group individuals may speak aloud what Carter is thinking, that is they will be in position as objects but speaking Carter's thoughts. Carter says they had a sleepless night afterwards. Dreams are usually rooted in real experience but can become fantastical or nightmarish. What could Carter have dreamed repeatedly that night?	• To empathize with the thoughts and feelings of archaeologists	*Thought-tracking* *Collective Role*	Chapter 6 of Carter and Mace's book opens with Carter's thoughts about this. He says he felt awe, embarrassment at breaking in, a sense of intrusion, exhilaration, suspense, an impulse to lift lids and break seals, joy, that he was adding to history, and so on.

(Continued)

Unit 6:   The Discovery of the Tomb of Tutankhamun *(Continued)*

Activity	Purpose/s	Drama strategy	Teacher guidance
7) **Different groups of four** Ask the children to create a piece of group movement that can be repeated (as a cycle). They should aim to make the movement interactive group movement rather than four individual pieces performed simultaneously. They will perform the piece of movement twice. They can add sounds or voice if they wish. When they have finished, they should rehearse. Afterwards show them as a performance carousel.	• To enable a collective, kinaesthetic representation of likely thoughts and fears • To enable them to work stylistically and symbolically, rather than only realistically.	***Movement/Dance Drama*** ***Performance Carousel***	This is creating dance but you may decide not to call it dance. Some boys particularly will be less likely to engage with movement if it is called dance. Let them experience and enjoy it and realize later maybe that this was dance … and that they enjoyed it!
Meanwhile the news of the discovery had spread like wildfire, and all sorts of extraordinary and fanciful reports were going abroad concerning it …			
8) **Whole class** Ask the class to stand in spaces. There were many rumours, for example, three aeroplanes have landed in the Valley and taken much of the treasure to an unknown place. Whoever opens tombs will be cursed. Ask the children to move around whispering and embellishing these rumours or they can make up new rumours of their own and spread them among each other. Carter invited officials to visit and inspect the site and see the treasure *in situ* and he sent a written account of events and findings to *The Times*.	• To engage with the way rumours get mixed with truth	***Rumours***	This is an opportunity to consider with the children why people spread rumours and what damage they can do. What damage could rumours do to Carter and the excavations? How might Carter best deal with rumours?

Unit 6: The Discovery of the Tomb of Tutankhamun

Activity	Purpose/s	Drama strategy	Teacher guidance
9) **In pairs** Ask the children to get into pairs and label themselves A and B. Then tell the As that they will be Carter and tell the Bs they are an Egyptian official who has been sent to find out what has been happening and check that the treasure is still there. A will lead B around the space, answering the official's questions, showing the antechamber, talking about events, and so on. Afterwards they can swap roles. This same paired activity could be done with different roles (some of which could be suggested by the children), for example: • English journalist and archaeologist friend of Carter and Carter • Egyptian and English archaeologists • Egyptian official and Egyptian journalist.	• To use working in role for questioning, explanation and reflection • To enable both children to experience being in both roles • To raise awareness that our speech alters when we have a different audience and purpose	*Improvisation*	If children decide to put on an Egyptian accent then let them as long as it does not distract them from the content of what they are saying. If it is done seriously and with commitment that is fine. If it is done for silly effect then tell them to drop the accent and focus on what they are saying. What different audiences did Carter have to communicate with about all this, for example, his family, Carnarvon (the funder), Egyptian officials, local people, the press, his workers, and so on? You might like to unravel with them why he would need to speak differently to various audiences, and why the children themselves do in real life.

Possible cross-curricular links

History

There will be a need to teach and learn more than was contained in the drama itself. This could be a good time to schedule a real museum visit or a virtual tour.

The drama is likely to stimulate a desire to find out more about Carter's exploration and discoveries. Authentic letters, diaries, photographs, documents, newspaper reports, may now be of increased interest to the children during and following the drama.

Geography

Look at a map of the Valley of the Tombs of the Kings. How would it differ from a map that Carter might have used?

Use the Internet to look at satellite photos of the site today.

English

Write a persuasive letter as Carter to Carnavon (before the discovery) trying to persuade him to keep funding the dig.

Use Carter's diary as a writing frame. Ask the children to imagine they are Carter and are redrafting and adding to what he has already written, based on their own experiences gained through the drama.

Write individually or in pairs, the account that Carter sent to *The Times*. (This could be started as a whole-class guided writing activity first.)

Write a diary entry as someone other than Carter, for example, a worker's diary, a journalist's diary, Carnarvon's imaginary diary, and so on.

Ask the children to imagine they are museum curators and the object they depicted in the drama (Activity 5) is going to be given to them to display. How will they display it to best advantage? Ask them to make the label and description that will be displayed with it.

ICT

Many museums offer recorded sound tours or virtual tours via the Internet. You could ask the children to create part of a soundtrack or virtual tour to accompany a visitor to a museum that is putting on an exhibition of some of the treasure.

Art

Study the objects. They are significant works of ancient Egyptian art, many decorated and painted. Use photographs of the actual objects to design and paint a picture of an object that could have been found, but was not, that is, create your own ancient Egyptian work of art or artefact that looks authentic. The tombs had been partly robbed. You could imagine that this is an object that was stolen by tomb robbers before Carter got there. You can use books and the Internet to research Ancient Egyptian designs and patterns first, to help you.

Music

Many museums have collections of music linked to Ancient Egypt. Listen and respond.

Ask the children to compose a piece of music (or a sound sequence using instruments) to tell the story of the discovery of the tomb, for example, repetitive digging, the 16 steps, chipping at the door, amazing discovery, regal splendour, and so on. Key moments need to be agreed first and then made clear through the music itself.

Citizenship

You could debate whether Carter is a tomb robber. Under what circumstances is it/is it not acceptable to enter a sacred tomb, remove the artefacts from the tomb and also from Egypt. The children could try to agree a set of guidelines and principles.

Unit 7: Leaving Home: Migration
(Years 5 and 6, ages 9–11 years)

Background information

This drama unit uses as its initial stimulus one evocative picture from a graphic novel created by Shaun Tan. It would be possible to augment this unit with Internet images (photographs, paintings, sculptures) of migrants and refugees from across the world and at different times in history. You could use these drama activities to teach history through drama by specifying a particular country or time. However, the universal human experience of migration may be more effectively approached if the time and place in this drama are not specified. You can start with the general universal human experience and then afterwards make links with particular times and places. Many children in schools are migrants or know migrants. This drama unit may in some way help non-migrant children appreciate the human elements and the immense personal challenges linked to migration and the importance of tolerance and inclusion, and migrant children may feel their personal circumstances have been better understood as a result of the whole-class drama experience. All characters in the book are nameless. The names Simon, Mary and Rebecca have been created for the drama. The brother, Peter, has also been added. This drama is not an enactment of the book but uses an image from it as a key stimulus and then actively explores some of the same themes as the book.

Resources

The Arrival by Shaun Tan, ISBN 0-7344-0694-0, published by Lothian Books (2006). This graphic novel is full of evocative images of migrant's stories. Having access to the book is highly recommended. The many images it contains of the departure, the journey, the arrival and settling in, would undoubtedly support and extend the drama below. Images may be found on Shaun Tan's website www.shauntan.net/books.html. This drama is built around the image entitled 'The Suitcase'. The image depicts a young couple standing by a wooden kitchen table with a closed suitcase on it and three chairs around it. They both are looking downwards. Their hands are rested on the suitcase. Hers are on top of his. Two hot cups of tea and a cracked teapot and documents are on the table. His hat hangs on the wall. On a shelf are a clock, paper bird, bottles and a cannister. Three pictures drawn by a young child hang from the wall. A casserole dish and spoon are in the background.

Sentence strips (jumbo size) and felt tip pens (one for each child).

Unit 7: Leaving Home: Migration

Activity	Purpose/s	Drama strategy	Teacher guidance
1) **Class circle (standing)** Explain to the children that you will make some statements that all start with the words, 'Move if ...'. If the statement applies to them personally then they should move to stand somewhere else in the circle. Move if: • you have moved house • you have been in a country and not been able to understand the language • you have been in a country where you could not understand the writing • you have felt as if you do not belong somewhere • you have not been able to make someone understand what you are saying • you have been on a long boat journey.	• To create a personal link with the drama theme to follow	***Drama Game***	You can add statements of your own. There are more sensitive statements that could be added in but you would need to decide their suitability for the children in your class. Move if: • you have ever had to leave someone you love • you have left behind a special possession you will never see again • you have ever had to spend the night in a place that is strange to you.
2) **Class circle (seated)** Make sure the class can all see the picture. Ask them not to talk to each other about the picture. They should just look at it alone, carefully, and 'wonder' to themselves. Then invite children to speak aloud what they are wondering, starting the sentence with, 'I wonder ...', for example, 'I wonder what is in the case'; 'I wonder why they aren't looking at each other', and so on. You may pass an object around the circle and the holder of the object is the one allowed to speak what he/she wonders, or you may decide that any child can speak out but they should try not to interrupt each other.	• To encourage visual engagement with the drama • To encourage close scrutiny of a picture • To stimulate curiosity • To share ideas and areas of curiosity		Their eyes will be drawn to the centre of the picture, but ask them to make sure that they look at all parts of the picture. There is nothing at all in this picture that does not have significance, so ask them to notice everything and to wonder. If you allow children to speak out at will, you may need to introduce the rule that they cannot speak twice in a row. This better ensures that everyone gets a turn and no one dominates.

(Continued)

131

Unit 7: Leaving Home: Migration (*Continued*)

Activity	Purpose/s	Drama strategy	Teacher guidance
3) **Class circle** Tell them that you will pretend to be the man in the picture. His name is Simon and he may have answers to some of their questions. Say that you will leave the circle and when you return you will be Simon and they can start to ask you questions. Answer any questions in role and get across some of the following key information: *Simon and Mary are married and love each other. They have one child, Rebecca. Simon has tried hard to get work but there are no jobs where they live. Simon's brother has gone by boat to another country to work and has written and suggested Simon joins him. Simon and Mary can only afford one single ticket. Simon intends to travel by ship. He hopes to stay with his brother Peter and to find a job and his own place to live and then send money for Mary to join him. He has been wondering about leaving for months and thinks it is the only way he can support his family in the future. It is not a decision he has reached lightly.*	• To give enough information for them to engage with a character and situation in the drama • To give answers to some of their questions in order to build the narrative	*Teacher in Role*	The children have been wondering about the picture but there comes a time when they want some 'real' information, or they may lose interest. The teacher in role can give enough information to get the drama started. You can play and develop the character of Simon in any way you wish and add further information. If there are questions you do not want to answer, you can say (in role) that you would prefer not to answer that question. The main thing is to stay in role and come across convincingly as a caring man who is reluctantly leaving his home, daughter and wife to find work in a strange country.
4) **Class circle** (sitting or standing) Ask them to look again at the picture. Tell them that every object in that room is important in some way. If the object could speak it could tell you why it is so important, for example, 'I am the clock and I am important because I am ticking away the time that Simon and Mary have left together before he leaves', 'I am the chair that Simon sits in and soon he will not be here to sit on me', and so on. In turn they have the opportunity to enter the circle (that represents the room in the picture) and place	• To build visually a shared and imagined environment • To actively support their understanding of personification	*Talking Objects* *Physical Theatre*	Very young children have no difficulty with animate objects, for example, the sun has a smiley face. Older children can have this openness reawakened through drama. Although the idea might seem a little odd to older children, as long as it is carried out seriously and with commitment it will work well as physical theatre.

Unit 7: Leaving Home: Migration

Activity	Purpose/s	Drama strategy	Teacher guidance
themselves as an object in the room, say what object they are and give a little information aloud as to why they are important. You may wish to model this first. Gradually several objects will enter and place themselves around the room. Only about eight people should do this, as a whole class would make the room too crowded. You can repeat the activity if you want to give other children a turn.	• To find out more about the characters and plot through inference		You may need to model the activity first and demonstrate your own committed approach to this activity and the length of contribution, that is, say what object you are and add a little information about yourself. Do not say much. Leave the audience wanting to know more.
Ask the objects to stay still in the room (but relaxing and reforming their positions if they are physically uncomfortable). Tell them that you will now pass through the room as Simon, who is walking around the room for the last time. As you pass by each object, it can speak to you and you can decide whether to respond to the object verbally or just non-verbally, for example, the clock might say, 'It is nearly time for you to go Simon'. Simon might just look at the clock or could say, 'It is nearly time for me to go. The minutes before I leave seem to be passing quickly'.	• To hold still a significant moment for reflection • To generate more knowledge and understanding of the character and plot	*Teacher in Role*	This gives you the opportunity to deepen their engagement through interaction with you in role as Simon. Your responding signals are that their contribution has worth and becomes part of the drama. They have shared ownership of the drama.
5) **Groups of 4** Simon has not made his decision to leave suddenly. There have been incidents over several months that have contributed to his decision to leave. You may wish to discuss the types of things that have happened that have ended up with Simon deciding to leave, for example, he lost his job, he cannot afford proper food for his family, they cannot pay the rent, and so on. Try to get and accept the children's ideas first before adding others if you need to.	• To actively consider some of the many factors that contribute to migration	*Small Group Play-making*	There is opportunity here for some extended discussion on the reasons for migration, or you may prefer to have this discussion before or after the drama lesson. Discussion about migration more fully at another time will help ensure that the drama remains fictitious, although relevant.

(Continued)

133

Unit 7: Leaving Home: Migration *(Continued)*

Activity	Purpose/s	Drama strategy	Teacher guidance
Ask them in groups of four to make a very short scene with Simon in it. They should create and enact an important moment that made Simon think it would be best to leave home and seek work elsewhere.	• To clearly communicate a reason contributing to migration		You will, of course, need to remain sensitive to the social issues that you may touch upon in the drama that may be directly relevant to children in your class (both migrant and native children).
• In each group one child (either male or female) will be Simon. • The scene must last no longer than a minute. • The scene should be given an agreed title. • The scene should start with a still image that then comes to life. • The scene should finish with a freeze-frame (so they need to agree the word/signal to all freeze on). • They should rehearse the scene at least once.	• To make clear the performance expectations • To ensure a unified approach that supports linking the group scenes		It is important to make your expectations clear. First, this helps the children feel secure and succeed, but also it supports better presentation and evaluation of their performance work. If you make the performance criteria clear it is easier for them and you to evaluate it fairly. Most importantly though:
After the scenes have been rehearsed tell them that each group will present their scene in turn without a pause between scenes. The groups not performing need to sit still and be quiet, as if they are also on stage but not yet in the spotlight. You can just move straight from scene to scene (after announcing each scene title) or you could ask the groups to start off on the ground and in slow motion move into the opening still image and then call out the title before performing. At the concluding freeze-frame they can melt back down to the floor in slow motion.	• To bring to life alternative, possible endings	*Performance Carousel*	• 'Was the performance effective?' • 'If it was/was not an effective performance, why?' • 'How might it be made even more effective?'
6) **Class circle (seated)** Give each child a strip of paper that they can write one sentence on in large writing (preferably with felt tip pen).	• To enable and model shared, collective writing in role	*Writing in Role*	When a child has only one sentence to write it is not a laborious and lengthy manipulative task (as writing can so often seem). They have time to spend crafting it for effect.

134

Unit 7: Leaving Home: Migration

Activity	Purpose/s	Drama strategy	Teacher guidance
Tell them that Simon left a letter for Mary that he knows she will find after he has left. He hopes the letter will cheer her up, when she finds it, and reassure her that all will end well and they will be reunited in better circumstances.	• To encourage written engagement with a character		They need to have some idea of the purpose of Simon's writing and its intended effect on the reader (Mary).
Each child is invited to write one sentence of Simon's letter (but not the opening or ending sentence).	• To build dramatic tension about what is hidden from view		
This activity needs to be carried out thoughtfully and silently. When they have written the sentence they should place the sentence strip in front of them with the writing face down.	• To signal that the sentence is finished		
Now every child has the opportunity in turn to read their sentence aloud as if they are Simon. Together a string of letter sentences will be shared aloud. Afterwards ask them if they can agree a possible order for these sentences. If they think they have a sentence that should be near the start of the letter, let them place it at the top of the class circle. If it is a sentence that fits better at the end of the letter, then they can place it at the bottom of the class circle. Then negotiate and discuss with them where all sentences can best fit, and elicit their shared reasoning for the relative placement of sentences. In the end you will have a sequence of sentences that becomes the letter Simon left Mary and can be read aloud again in one voice (probably yours).	• To stimulate and require literacy-based justification of sentence selection (letter structure and composition) • To link writing with dramatic activity • To participate in performing their writing • To hear their writing performed	*Collective Voice*	As long as they have answered the task, the letter will hang together as if written by one person. The discussion that takes place around why certain sentences are best placed in certain positions in relation to each other is a valuable, collaborative, literacy-based activity. Work at getting the children to listen to each other's literacy-based reasoning and come to agreement. The fact they own one of the sentences gives them a personal stake in the outcome and helps keep them engaged with the process.
7) **Class circle (standing)** Enter the centre of the circle and tell them that you will be Mary. You have just found and read the letter. Ask them to speak aloud what Mary is thinking at this moment. Children can either speak spontaneously, while trying not to speak	• To encourage empathy	*Teacher in Role* *Teacher in Role*	They have the advantage of already knowing well what the letter contains because of the previous activity. This is an opportunity for them to share ownership of the possible impact of the letter that they collectively wrote.

(Continued)

135

Unit 7: Leaving Home: Migration *(Continued)*

Activity	Purpose/s	Drama strategy	Teacher guidance
at the same time, or you could pass an object around the circle and the person holding the object is the only one empowered to speak at the time.	• To share ownership of a main character	*Thought-tracking*	
A different way to do this is 'on the move', where the child who speaks the thought walks past Mary and speaks her thought when they are near her and then arrives at a different place in the class circle.	• To link thought and physical theatre	*Passing Thoughts*	Passing thoughts is just thought-tracking but with children moving dramatically past a character to present their thoughts.
A third possibility is that someone enters, stands close to Mary, or touches her on the shoulder, and then speaks her thought. Others then enter and also spatially and/or physically connect in some way with the image already there. A sort of tableau will gradually emerge.	• To link thought and image	*Tableau*	Creating a tableau of thoughts makes physical the thought and keeps it for us visually. We end up with the thoughts clustered together as a tableau. It would be possible to let thoughts come and go, that is, break free and then re-enter the tableau.
8) **Groups of four** Simon's future and the end of this drama is uncertain. The outcome lies in the hands of the children. • Does Simon find work in another country where he cannot yet speak the language? • If so, is the work well enough paid or is he exploited? • Does he find a home for Mary and Rebecca to come to? • Does he make friends in the new country? • Can he earn enough to send for his family? • Does he experience kindness and/or hostility? • Does he find himself in a worse situation, that is, unemployed in a strange country and away from his family?	• To give ownership and responsibility for the plot to the children • To focus attention on a range of possible issues Simon will face • To raise awareness that story 'endings' in real life are not always happy endings	*Small Group Play-making*	Simon's future is unknown. The children have the possibility of making it a positive one but not without having considered that it might not be. Several drama lessons could be spent exploring how Simon copes in his new country of residence, and letters home or a diary would be a linked possibility.

Unit 7: Leaving Home: Migration

Activity	Purpose/s	Drama strategy	Teacher guidance
• Does he manage to stay with his brother and, if so, does this work out alright? • Can he make himself understood in a country where he does not speak the language? and so on.			
Ask the children in groups of four to prepare a short realistic scene (no more than a minute) that lets us just glimpse how the future might turn out for Simon. You can use the questions as prompts if you wish or you could ask different groups to focus on different aspects of the future, for example, housing, work, language, family, health, friendship, communication, and so on. Give them about five minutes to prepare the scene (which should last no longer than a minute).	• To bring alive several possible alternative outcomes for consideration		You only want a glimpse so do not let them offer long performances. Get across that less can most certainly equate to more in drama, and it is quality not quantity that you are seeking.
Then let each group show the scenes, possibly as a performance carousel (see Activity 5).	• To create a whole-class performance	*Performance Carousel*	
An alternative is that the groups prepare a scene for Simon (teacher in role) to walk into and improvise within, for example, Simon walks into a job interview that is either friendly or hostile.	• To witness a character's spontaneous response	*Improvisation*	If Simon is having difficulties in his new country it might be possible for the children to offer him advice (through teacher in role as Simon) as to how he might be able to deal with some of his problems. Maybe arriving together at three key pieces of advice for Simon would be a way of focusing their discussion around helping him to settle.
Another alternative is to ask the groups to present two still images. One will show the ideal ending for Simon and the other the worst-case scenario. These contrasting images can be presented as still or moving images, either realistically or as a dream/nightmare.	• To get all to consider extreme possible outcomes	*Image Theatre*	

(Continued)

137

Unit 7: Leaving Home: Migration *(Continued)*

Activity	Purpose/s	Drama strategy	Teacher guidance
You could ask them to present two contrasting still images and move stylistically between them, or you could ask them to create symbolic movement that is repeated and changes from ideal to worst-case scenario and back again repeatedly. Troubled dreams are often vivid and repeated dreams. Suitable background music could be a very effective addition.	• To give opportunity to focus on and create symbolic movement • To encourage focused discussion aimed at devising (selection, justification, reasoning, synthesis, evaluation)	*Dance/Drama* *Movement*	There has been much emphasis on the written and spoken word in this drama unit. However non-verbal and non-written communication can often express and communicate aspects of human behaviour and thinking differently, and often more effectively.

Possible cross-curricular links

Geography/History

Migration is not always related to war. It is worth exploring with the children why different waves of migration have occurred. This unit of work can be linked and used directly to be about real waves of migration that are historical or current, for example, Jews in World War II, Afghan and Iraqi refugees now, Polish workers, and so on.

English

There is much opportunity for letter writing between Mary and Simon.

Either character could keep a personal diary.

Internet searches will reveal authentic and moving refugee poetry and stories.

The alphabet depicted in the pictures in the book is fictitious.

Anne Frank's *Diary* could be interesting to link with this unit.

The children could have fun inventing and teaching each other some bits of a new and imaginary language.

Mathematics

Codes and decoding: Individually or in pairs the children could create their own alphabet and written language that others could try to decode.

Art

In Shaun Tan's book there are children's drawings from time to time that almost act as a child's view of events. The children could draw events as if they are the child in the drama (Rebecca). These could form a storyboard.

The art work in the book is often in the style of comics (storyboard) and is sometimes cinematic. It would be possible to take a Shaun Tan image and imagine it extended. Incidents and events that happen in the drama could then be drawn in the style of Shaun Tan, as if they are additions or extensions of the actual book.

PSHE

There are many emotional aspects and social issues within this drama that can be directly followed up through PSHE, for example, inclusion, tolerance, single parenting, unemployment, and so on.

Citizenship/Media

What does Simon need to know about when he arrives to live in another country? How will he find out? Making a propaganda film for new citizens to an imaginary country can be fun and enlightening. This could be done through further drama, with different groups devising and then seamlessly presenting various scenes from an imaginary information film (transport, health, education, leisure, work, and so on). These scenes actually could be filmed.

What helps migrants settle into another country? How can we help?

Unit 8: The Listeners
(Year 6, ages 10–11 years)

Background information

This lesson explores the poem, 'The Listeners,' by Walter de la Mare and uses it as a creative stimulus. This poem can be accessed on www.web-books.com/classics/poetry/anthology/DeLaMare/Listeners.htm. The drama enables the children actively to study the text and themes, and use these as a springboard for imagining, devising and extending the characters, setting and plot. The lesson starts with a strong literacy focus and moves into drama. It is not necessary to carry out all the activities but they have been designed to build on what has gone before, so it may be best not to mix up the order of activities.

> *On a moonlit night, a man arrives by horse, at an apparently deserted house in a forest. He dismounts and knocks on the door several times. No one answers and yet before leaving he calls out to 'phantom listeners,' asking them to 'tell them' he came as promised but that no one had answered. He then rides away again. The poem is tantalizingly ambiguous and the reader is left with many unanswered questions in relation to both the plot and main character.*

Unit 8: The Listeners

Activity	Purpose/s	Drama strategy	Teacher guidance
1) *Outside the house/in the forest* **Class circle (seated)** Ask the children to close their eyes as you read the poem to them. As they listen they should try to visualize the place where the poem is set. Ask them to keep their eyes closed afterwards for a while and keep it as a picture in their mind's eye. They may imagine additional detail beyond that mentioned in the poem. Ask them to let their mind's eye move around the picture and notice detail. What do they 'see' and how could they describe it? Trying not to speak at the same time as each other, tell them that they can say aloud what they can 'see' and add a little detail, for example, 'I can see the long shadows of the trees in the silvery moonlight' rather than just 'I can see shadows'.	• To encourage a focused, visual and auditory engagement with text • To give time for the visual image to linger and be enhanced • To give opportunity for the sharing of ideas that can help build up a more vivid shared and imagined setting	*Visualization* *Shared and Guided Visualization*	Listening to a poem and trying to visualize from it, rather than reading it first, can support visual engagement and aid memory. The term, 'mind's eye' may need explanation, possibly as 'a picture inside your head'. Often we rush children between activities. Linger. Give them enough time to think and let the imagination wander. If you join in the activity yourself, you will get a better visual understanding of the shared setting and better sense when to stop this activity and move on. You can also contribute to the activity as a co-participant.
2) **Groups of four** Ask them to look at the text with their group. Each group will search through the poem and each group will underline one of the following (in larger classes you may need to have more than one group focusing on the same sense): Words that suggest: 1. sound/silence, for example, knocking, said, and so on 2. movement/stillness, for example, knocking, champ'd, and so on	• To encourage analysis and discussion about specific words • To make links between words and the senses		This is a literacy rather than a drama activity. Encourage the children to share and discuss with their groups. They could have one group scribe or do the activity individually or in pairs within the group and then share and agree.

Unit 8: The Listeners

Activity	Purpose/s	Drama strategy	Teacher guidance
3. light/dark, for example, moonlit, grey 4. smell, for example, grasses 5. touch/texture, for example, the knock on door.			
They might suggest other imaginary, sensory details the author could have added relating to the man, the house or to the surroundings, for example, the smell of the horse's sweat, the sound of the man's breathing and heartbeat, the dry roof of his mouth, the splintered wood beneath his knuckles.	• To give opportunity for co-authorship		Re-visualizing the setting and then asking them to travel through it in their imaginations (maybe as the man) with an eye, an ear, nose, fingers, tongue in turn can result in interesting and vivid suggestions. Linking senses to emotion is a literacy device you might wish to mention, for example, the smell or taste of fear.
3) **Same groups of four** Read the poem to the class again. This time, when you reach a 'sense' word they have selected, ask them to read it out aloud with you. It will become evident that some words are multi-sensory and will be spoken aloud by more than one group at a time, for example, knocking might be called out by the movement and sound and touch group.	• To make public the links between words and the senses • To highlight that one word can link to more than one sense	*Choral Speaking*	This is again a literacy activity rather than a drama activity. If some single words have been selected for more than one sense, then draw attention to this if necessary.
4) **Same groups of four** Ask the 'senses' groups to select from among their words. Then give the various groups the following instructions. a) **Sound/silence group:** Prepare a sound effects collage that will be performed to the rest of the class (who will have their eyes closed as it is performed). They will need to think in advance where to best position themselves in relation to their 'blind' audience. They should be able to repeat it seamlessly if required.	• To encourage group co-operation and collaboration • To build sound/words association • To build trust and care (a 'blind' audience feels vulnerable).	*Sound/Collage Performance*	Children often are so busy devising that they forget to take consider the audience. Before the performance they need to think about the audience and how to ensure maximum impact, for example, would it be most effective to seat the 'blind' audience in the centre and move among them … or around them … or should the performers be static in the centre and perform outwards, and so on. What is likely to be most effective and why?

(Continued)

Unit 8: The Listeners (Continued)

Activity	Purpose/s	Drama strategy	Teacher guidance
b) **Movement/stillness:** Use some 'movement' words from the poem as the stimulus for a piece of group movement, which will then be performed. They should be able to repeat the collective movement seamlessly if required.	• To build movement/words association kinaesthetically	*Movement Performance*	
c) **Light/dark:** Ask each person in the group to use alliteration to extend one of the light/dark words, for example, 'milky, misty, moonlit'. Once each person has a cluster of alliterated words then they should be playful with them as a group to develop a voice collage or piece of movement that will be performed to the rest of the class. They should be able to repeat it seamlessly if required.	• To create and reinforce alliteration aurally and/or visually and kinaesthetically	*Voice/Word Collage Performance* *Movement Performance*	There are good examples of alliteration in the poem, that is, 'forest's ferny floor' and 'silence slipped softly' that their attention should be drawn to.
d) **Smell, for example, grasses:** Ask each person in the group to create a short descriptive phrase evoking an odour linked to the poem, for example, 'damp, rotting ferns' and 'the sharp smell of horse-sweat'. Once each person has a short phrase then they should add exaggerated gestures to accompany each word in the phrase. They should be able to repeat it seamlessly if required.	• To link words and gesture to communicate and reinforce meaning	*Voice/Word Collage Performance* *Movement Performance*	Try to get the children to exaggerate gestures that link to each word. You may need to model this. They will tend to make gestures smaller than required if they do not see a demonstration and have not done this before. The gestures are to be big and symbolic rather than realistic. Slow motion gesturing might be helpful.

144

Activity	Purpose/s	Drama strategy	Teacher guidance
e) **Touch/texture:** Each person in the group should prepare a journey for a partner (who will have their eyes closed). They will be guiding a partner safely to touch objects in the room and providing a narrative that suggests they are in the setting of the poem, for example, 'This is the door that the traveller knocked on. Your hand is exactly where his hand was when he knocked'. Material (curtains), glass (windows), metal (radiators) can all be used to help the 'blind' partner to believe they are in the imaginary setting of the poem. This group can take a few class members each on the sensory tour afterwards.	• To encourage imaginative narrative • To develop trust and care (a 'blind' partner feels vulnerable) • To use tactile experience to support imagined experience	*Sensory Journey/Tour*	You can ask the children simply to use the objects and furnishings in the room or you could gather a box of useful items that might be helpful to them, for example, fern leaves, ivy, a horseshoe, a piece of velvet, a piece of leather, lace, a key, a hip flask and so on.
5) **Same groups of four (paired together)** Although the 'senses' groups are working separately for Activity 4 (above) they can be linked afterwards to create other linked performances, for example: • a sound collage group can work afterwards with a movement group and provide the soundtrack for their movement • a sound effects group can attach itself to enhance the sensory tour • voice and sound collage groups can work at integrating their performances	• To give experience of reworking an existing performance to accommodate new stimuli • To focus on a multi-sensory performance	*Improvised Performance*	This activity gives an opportunity to change and extend an existing performance piece. To work experimentally with a performance is exciting and requires flexibility and compromise and a willingness to share ownership. The combined performances symbolically reunite the senses. This can be further emphasized through simultaneous performances.

(Continued)

Unit 8: The Listeners (*Continued*)

Activity	Purpose/s	Drama strategy	Teacher guidance
6) **The house (outside)** **Class ideally seated on the floor in a horseshoe shape** Look again at the poem. What do we *know* about the house exterior? For example the window sills are leaf-fringed. There is a turret, and so on. There may be other details that we can add that the poet did not, for example, a heavy brass door knocker that is no longer shiny.			
In turn give the children the opportunity to enter the space and use their bodies to portray parts of the house exterior, for example, become the window sill, the doorstep, and so on. In turn, as they enter, they each say what they are and a sentence or two about themselves, for example, 'I am the doorstep. No one has stepped on me for many years. I am worn and old'. Gradually a house will appear that has been created collectively.	• To create a set physically • To learn/imagine more about the house • To create a shared, experiential understanding of personification	*Physical Theatre* *Talking Objects* *Tableau*	You may need to model this first. Children not used to doing this are likely to laugh at the idea to begin with but keep them serious about it and you will be pleasantly surprised at how intrigued the children become as the house emerges.
7) **The traveller approaches** They should stay in position as the house. Tell them that you will now approach the house as the traveller. You will approach twice. The first time they should try to make you turn away by what they say and the second time they should entice you towards the house by what they say. They should try not to interrupt each other or talk at the same time, for example, the leaves on the window sill might say, 'Go away from this place. I am hiding what you must not see. Be warned!' Or second time maybe, 'Come closer traveller and look through the window. You will like what you see'. When you have arrived as the traveller at the door, pause.	• To raise the level of dramatic tension • To continue to explore shared personification	*Teacher in Role* *Collective Role*	Children who have got themselves into tiring positions need to be able to come out of position for a few seconds and then get back into it. It's worth suggesting that they get into positions that can be sustained comfortably.

Unit 8: The Listeners

Activity	Purpose/s	Drama strategy	Teacher guidance
Ask them to speak out loud, in turn, the traveller's thoughts at this key moment, that is, just about to knock for the first time, for example, 'I wonder if they are here?'		*Thought-tracking* *Collective Role*	When the children speak the traveller's thoughts it is perfectly acceptable for him to have contradictory thoughts but you may decide to suggest they try to keep the listener's thoughts consistent as they belong to the one character. This requires better listening and concentration.
To bring this to a close, knock on the imaginary door and shout, 'Tell them I came and no one answered, that I kept my word'.			
8) **The main character and the plot** **Whole-class rectangle (standing)** The poem offers very little information. Clearly define three adjacent spaces in the room as:	• To create a visual, auditory and kinaesthetic 'inter-thinking' frame	*Improvisation*	If this lesson is taking place in a hall with floor markings, then the thirds of a netball pitch make ideal divisions for the three areas of this physical 'thinking frame': 1. What we know. 2. What we think we know. 3. What we want to know.

1. What we know.	2. What we *think* we know.	3. What we *want* to know.

Activity	Purpose/s	Drama strategy	Teacher guidance
In turn each child has the opportunity to physically place themselves in an appropriate area (1, 2 or 3) and voice a statement commencing with the word, 'we', for example:	• to assess present knowledge and understanding, and where the children's interest lies		This same activity could be done by writing in columns rather than by each person physically moving into a space, but the effect of doing it physically, visually and with voice is that it stylistically creates a piece of improvised theatre.
'We *know* the man has a horse.' (1) 'We *think* we know he has travelled a long way.' (2) 'We *want* to know who he made a promise to.' (3)			

(Continued)

Unit 8: The Listeners (*Continued*)

Activity	Purpose/s	Drama strategy	Teacher guidance
9) *Inside the house* **Ask them to turn (still standing) in a class rectangle or circle facing inwards** Tell them that they can now see inside the house. It is as if they are the walls of the house. Ask them to use their hands to create a peep-hole to look through. Ask them to speak aloud what they can 'see' in the uninhabited house. They should try not to speak simultaneously. Recall with them what we know from the poem is there already, for example, a staircase. They can add items of furniture and objects not mentioned in the poem, for example, 'I can see a mirror on the wall'. Gradually the inside of the house will be created. Usually someone will mention a picture or photograph or tapestry. Join in yourself and if no child suggests any images such as these then you can contribute one to lead into the next activity, for example, I can see a big painting hanging next to the staircase.	• To build a shared, imagined environment • To ensure a smooth link into the next activity	*Improvisation* *Teacher in Role*	An alternative here would be to let them enter the circle and become the objects in the house but this may be too similar to Activity 7. This could enable you, however, to invite questioning of the objects to find out more about the past. Do not offer your contribution at the start unless you need to. Let the children start and you hold back a while.
10) *Finding out more about the past* **Groups of four** Tell them that there are several pictures (or photos or tapestries) to be found in the house and the traveller is in each one at a different point of time in the past. The pictures may help us learn a little more about the traveller and help us piece together past parts of the plot. Ask the groups to make a still image of one of the pictures in the house and to give it a one-sentence title.	• To build together the character and plot	*Still Image*	An alternative to creating paintings of the past might come from being alert to the children's ideas offered, for example, a mirror can offer the opportunity to make reflections of scenes the mirror has witnessed in the past. A book or letter in the room can become an opportunity to all create sentences from it and sequence them. If you can use the children's ideas to move the drama on then this is preferable, as it offers them more ownership of the drama.

Unit 8: The Listeners

Activity	Purpose/s	Drama strategy	Teacher guidance
Once they have created the image they should practise starting as a still group on the floor and then moving into the image in slow motion, freezing at the same moment and then one person will call out the title. After a few seconds they will melt back onto the floor in slow motion and be still simultaneously.	• To ensure a consistent approach to the group presentation	*Freeze-frame*	You may find it helps to tell them to grow into the still image to a count of 5 silent seconds 'in their heads'. Then hold the image for 5 seconds … call the title out aloud … hold it again for a further 5 seconds and then melt down again in 5 seconds.
Whole class together in groups Once all groups have rehearsed the above they will be presented in an uninterrupted sequence, one group at a time. When one group has finished and is still, the next group starts to move.	• To link group performances seamlessly into one continuous whole-class performance	*Performance Carousel*	Insist on total stillness and silence from all but the performing group. Ensure that there is no shuffling or chatting during this 'performance carousel' as it breaks the theatrical effect.
Afterwards you can decide together the likely chronological order of the pictures and, if you wish, repeat the carousel in this agreed order.		*Performance Carousel*	
You can invite questioning of the characters in each picture by the rest of the class. The characters in the picture should answer in role.		*Hot-seating*	You may wish to restrict questioning to only one question of each character or maybe say that no one can ask more than one question.

Possible cross-curricular links

English

By the end of the drama a semi-complete story will have emerged. This could be used to create a range of writing opportunities:

Poetry: Return to the poem and write additional lines that link to the plot created through the drama. The additional lines need to fit in seamlessly, as if Walter de la Mare had added them himself!

'Stopping by Woods on a Snowy Evening' by Robert Frost, is an interesting poem to look at in conjunction with 'The Listeners'. It can be found on ww.emule.com/poetry/?page=poem&poem=2944. It can be linked to provide the part of the plot preceding the traveller's arrival at the house. The children could create a third poem that focuses on the traveller on his journey back home after calling fruitlessly at the house.

Scriptwriting: Think back to one of the pictures hanging on the wall. Give each character one line only and script the lines using an existing playscript as a model writing frame.

Story openings: Create just the opening sentence (or paragraph) of this drama-story. You could do this in the third person or as the traveller … or as the house … or as a phantom listener!

Art/English

Use the poem itself to create a picture that is based only on textual references. You can enlarge the sentences of the poem on a photocopier, cut them out and stick them at the relevant part of the picture.

Geography

What might lead to houses becoming derelict? Are there local derelict houses? Why … or why not?

What materials are the local houses built of? Are any specific to the geographical area?

Science

What materials might the house in the forest have been built of? Which materials would decay or wear first?

History

What clues would you look for to help you decide the age of a house?

PSHE

Why are promises important? Can you think of times when you have kept (or broken) your word? Is it always possible to keep a promise?

GLOSSARY OF DRAMA STRATEGIES AND CONVENTIONS

Collective Role/Collective Voice

A group or whole class of children speak in turn as one character. This shares the ownership of the character and responsibility for a character's development. They have to listen carefully to each other to be sure that the contributions fit with the one character.

Conscience Alley (or Decision Alley/Thought Tunnel)

The class divides into two lines facing each other with a corridor down the centre through which a character can walk. As the character walks between the lines, one side tries to persuade him/her to take one course of action and, the other, the opposite course of action. Or one line gives the pros and the other the cons. Each person has opportunity to speak to the character when he/she is standing nearest them. The character can join one line to indicate a decision has been made in accordance with that line. The line can be made longer if people break away once they have spoken and add themselves on to the end of the line.

Eavesdropping

A character (often the teacher in role) listens in to scenes, as if they are eavesdropping on them. This can be done in an exaggerated way with hand to ear. The rest of the class also sits still and listens until it is their group's turn to be eavesdropped upon, while the others listen.

Freeze-frame

A freeze-frame is made by in-role action being halted mid-flow to a given signal, for example, the teacher calling 'Freeze'. Those in the scene need to then remain very still, as if frozen. At a further agreed signal, for example, 'Action', the freeze-frame can be broken or thawed, and the action can then carry on again.

Image Theatre

This involves presenting a series of still images. Often the images are contrasting, for example, hopes/fears, ideal/reality. The groups might move between the images in slow motion or back and forth between the two. Time may be given to discuss the comparisons and consider what steps would be needed by a character to move from one situation portrayed to the other, for example, how to get from fear to hope or from the reality to the ideal.

Mantle of the Expert

This involves children taking on the role of experts, usually involved in taking on a significant task for an imaginary external customer. For example, the children might be in role as designers with a brief that they are fulfilling for an imaginary development company.

Passing Thoughts

This is thought-tracking 'on the move'. A character stands in the centre and in turn the whole class can pass by the character and speak the character's thoughts aloud. Alternatively they can pass by the character and offer advice or reassurance at a key moment.

Performance Carousel

This is a theatrical way of seeing the linked work of several groups in sequence. All groups imagine they are on stage waiting still and silent for their spotlight turn. One at a time seamlessly each group performs, while the rest are still and silent. The groups might move into a still image starting position and all freeze at the end of their group performance before melting down into stillness between group scenes.

Physical Theatre

This involves performing in ways that use the body as objects, properties, scenery, and so on, rather than just as people. The body is used in a versatile and creative way to become whatever the drama requires.

Ritual

This involves everyone carrying out repeated agreed actions, words or sounds for a significant purpose within the drama. Ritual makes actions and words significant and important and might give them symbolic meaning.

Rumours

In a short amount of time everyone makes up and spreads a rumour among the whole class. Some rumours may be true and others may not. Good false rumours are not easily distinguishable from truth. Afterwards the rumours may be gathered for collective consideration. This quickly creates many plot possibilities.

Sensory Journey/Tour

One person has their eyes closed. Their partner guides them around the drama space, talking to them and leading them on an apparent journey in another environment linked to the drama. They can use touch, texture, sound and words to feed into the experience for the blindfolded person. The partner may be led by the elbow or just by verbal instruction with no touch.

Small Group Play-making

This is self-explanatory, other than to say that the group usually comprises up to four children and the play they make is usually a short scene. Often the class divides into groups for this activity based on a theme. They usually bring the scenes back together afterwards to show each other (possibly using Performance Carousel).

Sound Collage

This involves building a setting or atmosphere creatively through sound effects. The sounds are usually made from the body or objects found in the room. Sounds can be repeated, overlap, be loud, quiet, and so on. The activity is usually done by a group and links to a purpose within the drama. Often the sound collage is presented to an audience who keep their eyes closed.

Still Image

A still image is of course a still picture. It is not necessarily the same as a freeze-frame. A freeze-frame is a type of still image. We might ask children to make a still image and this would involve a creative devising process, whereas a freeze-frame is not planned, the children just 'freeze'.

Tableau

A tableau is another type of still image. It often ends up involving the whole class. It usually is built up gradually, with the addition of one or two people at a time.

Talking Objects

This involves the children portraying themselves as objects in a scene. The objects usually enter the scene one at a time. They can speak, tell you about themselves and characters and events they have witnessed. They can be questioned and can talk to each other. Characters might pass by the talking objects and the objects might speak to the character or about the character. Also, the objects can speak to each other.

Teacher in Role

This involves the teacher taking a role in the drama. They will signal clearly to the children when they are in or out of role and may use a piece of costume or prop to make this clear. The teacher only stays in role for as long as is necessary to the drama. They do not need to act, just present a set of attitudes with seriousness and consistency.

Teacher as Narrator

This involves the teacher telling, or telling back, parts of the drama as if he/she is a storyteller. This may be used to gather and share what has happened in the drama so far and to move the drama forward in time so that it does not get stuck. It enables the teacher to model narrative storytelling.

Thought-tracking

This involves speaking the inner thoughts of a character out loud and is often an opportunity offered to the whole class at a key moment. It may be that a child gets an opportunity to speak the character's thoughts aloud when the teacher is passing nearest to that child. Sometimes a touch on the shoulder is used as a signal that it is their turn to speak the thoughts of the character.

Voice Collage

This is usually carried out by a group or class. A voice collage is built up (maybe spontaneously or maybe rehearsed) that links to the drama. It involves using only voices. The voices can speak words, make sounds, repeat, overlap, interrupt, and so on. When voice collages are being performed it is usually most effective if the audience have their eyes closed.

REFERENCES

Arts Council England (ACE) (2002) *Drama in Schools: Second Edition*. London: Arts Council England.

Baldwin, P. (2004) *With Drama in Mind: Real Learning in Imagined Worlds*. Stafford: Network Educational Press.

Boal, A. (2002) *Games for Actors and Non-Actors*. London: Routledge.

Department for Education and Skills (DfES) (2006) *Renewed Primary Framework for Literacy and Mathematics*. www.standards.dfes.gov.uk/primary framework/ (accessed 20 February 2008).

Department for Education and Skills (DfES) (May 2003a) *Excellence and Enjoyment: A Strategy for Primary Schools*. London: DfES. (Ref DfES 0377/2003).

Department for Education and Skills (DfES) (2003b) *Drama Objectives Bank*. London: DfES. www.standards.dfes.gov.uk/secondary/keystage3/downloads/en_dramaobjs032103bank.pdf

Department for Education and skills (DfES) (2004) *Speaking, Listening, Learning: Working with Children in Key Stages 1 and 2*. London: DfES.

Downing, D., Johnson, F. and Kaur, S. (2003) *Saving a Place for the Arts? A Survey of the Arts in Primary Schools*. LGA research report 41. London: NFER.

Heathcote, D. and Bolton, G. (1995) *Drama for Learning: Dorothy Heathcote's Mantle of the Expert Approach to Education*. London: Heinemann.

Norfolk County Council and National Drama (NCC and ND) (2007) *Drama for Learning and Creativity (D4LC)*. Norwich: Norfolk County Council and National Drama.

Pullman, P. (2004) The *Guardian* Tuesday 30th March, http//education.guardian.co.uk/egweekly/story/0,5500,1180330,00,html

RECOMMENDED READING

Ackroyd, J. (2001) *Drama Lessons for 5 to 11 Year Olds*. London: David Fulton.

Baldwin, P. (2004) *With Drama in Mind: Real Learning in Imagined Worlds*. Stafford: Network Educational Press.

Baldwin, P. and Fleming, K. (2002) *Teaching Literacy Through Drama: Creative Approaches*. London: RoutledgeFalmer.

Bowell, P. and Heap, B. (2001) *Planning Process Drama*. London: David Fulton.

Dickinson, R., Neelands, J. and Shenton Primary School (2006) *Improve Your Primary School Through Drama*. London: David Fulton.

Fleming, M. (1998) *Starting Drama Teaching*. London: David Fulton.

Neelands, J., and Goode, T. (2000) *Structuring Drama Work*. Cambridge: Cambridge University Press.

Toye, N. and Prendiville, F. (2000) *Drama and Traditional Story in the Early Years*. London: Routledge.

Toye, N. and Prendiville, F. (2007) *Speaking and Listening Through Drama*. London: Sage Publications.

Winston, J. and Tandy, M. (1998) *Beginning Drama 4–11*. London: David Fulton.